Ashten is a truth-teller. A speaker of the secrets that are held close to the broken-hearted. In his advancement for empowerment, he seeks to blow open the locked doors that shelter the predatory people that hide behind them; preying on the vulnerable. As a nurse and a Master Reiki Practitioner, he feels blessed to journey with people in their weakest moments. He is uplifting and hopeful and with intentions for the healing of the wounded he sets forth each day. He hopes that this book – his story – will offer catharsis to those who need it and enlightenment for those who had little or no clue of the extent of grief another soul can sorrow through.

Merlyn, Peggy and Ron, Charlaine – for keeping me alive, thank you.

Tina: the starlight that led me home to myself.

To all my brothers and sisters who have suffered under the weight of secrets and shame, I am your ally.

And to my good doctor, Amy, I have found profound peace in loving you – winky face.

Ashten Leverick

EXCRUCIATE

AUSTIN MACAULEY PUBLISHERS™

LONDON • CAMBRIDGE • NEW YORK • SHARJAH

Ordering Information
Quantity sales: Special discounts are available on quantity purchases by corporations, associations, and others. For details, contact the publisher at the address below.

Publisher's Cataloging-in-Publication data
Leverick, Ashten
Excruciate

ISBN 9781649795939 (Paperback)
ISBN 9781649795946 (ePub e-book)

Library of Congress Control Number: 2023903708

www.austinmacauley.com/us

First Published 2023
Austin Macauley Publishers LLC
40 Wall Street
33rd Floor, Suite 3302
New York, NY 10005 USA

mail-usa@austinmacauley.com
+1 (646) 5125767

With gratitude and humility, I acknowledge that I live and work on the traditional unceded territories of the Musqueam, Squamish, and Tsleil-Waututh peoples.

Table of Contents

"They say time heals all wounds. It is not so for me. My wound gapes open, angry, and obscene. It is a fungating cancerous mass that swells and oozes – smearing its putrid pus along the landscape of my life. Time has allowed only for that. For it to embed its stink more deeply into my flesh; like a virus, it penetrates my cells and copulates, twisting the strands of my DNA into morbid complexities until I am no longer me entirely. And I wonder how long until its corruption of my being overtakes me wholly."

Who are they?

"Those who speak of time as a medicine. A poultice for a wound that nourishes the cell beds and encourages the proliferation of new tissue into life. They know not what they speak of, if that is, their speaking was meant for my ears too.

She is my virus. A chronic disease that punctuates my days with an acuity of pain, an unrelenting mental confusion; like Lyme disease, she creeps under my flesh and pronounces herself in idiopathic ways that baffle me and tease me – leading me farther from myself with her twists of symptoms pointing fingers in different directions…until the dizziness of her torment leaves me wandering far off course and thinking that this really is a physical death I am facing. She is like a neurotoxin; my mind and my brain become severed from each other and I feel sensations that are not real to this moment. She is a demon virus dogging me. And I wonder if it will haunt me for all of my days."

How did this happen? How did this sickness come upon you?

"I wonder…in knowing, will the antidote come to be revealed? As with all infections, there is a required port of entry. Through this, the critters crawl to the blood, the cell walls, the tissue. She has entered the marrow of me. There 'She' resides, in the place where the liquid of life is birthed and formed. That is the outcome."

But how did She get there? Where was her entrance into the sacred part of you?

"In three words, her lips and her tongue, moving on her perfect sharp teeth, edges just enough to show a wink of danger when she curled Her lips in Her coy way to say, 'This is heat, this is raw, this is the light bite on your bottom lip that draws blood; an appetizer for the wet warmth that is to come, this all of your sex and all of your soul.'" She said, 'This is fantasy.' And there was Her entrance. That was the portal that leads to my death. 'This is fantasy.'"

Chapter 1
Lost in My Mind

"I think I should call the story 'Excruciate'…but then I really shouldn't call it a 'story' should I?"

Why not a story?

"Well, if I call it a story, doesn't that denote a falseness? A fiction to it? I worry it takes away the realness of it, to call it a 'story.'"

But a story can be real. We commonly hear it don't we – in recent history, dot dot dot. Recent his-story. History is real. Your story, it is real?

Humph. "It is real. It's the kind of real that rapes your entire sense of reality. Is so fucking far beyond what you expect to have happened that it's un-real. It's the ultimate unreality. And it happened nonetheless. The unreality is the reality in which I lived. And to which I fear I will return. The problem is…ha, 'the' problem. As if there is only one. OK, so a problem is: I don't know where to begin."

What if you just begin at the beginning?

"Right. The beginning. I suppose there was one of those. But so much of it just swirls around in my mind, just above my head; I can see it. If I close my eyes or I let my vision blur out of focus on just exactly what is right in front of me, there are numbers and words and images flashing all around the upper periphery of my vision. Dates and whispers and our bodies and her hands and her nails and her rings and her wedding ring and the doorknob glinting as it reflects sunshine streaming in from the window and my god I hope no one just walked by the window and saw this, this, what *is* going on in here; and is the door locked my god imagine if someone walked in right now; and there are smells too, Vanilla perfume and cherry Chapstick and peach gum and Export-A green, standard size, in a twenty-five pack. And it all sounds so young, doesn't it? So boy meets girl. Until the part about the wedding ring and the Export-A green and then maybe someone would clue in that this isn't a girl I am talking about…You see?"

Do I see what?

"I get so lost in it all. I ramble on about the flying images circling my skull like so many galaxies in orbit. I confound myself when I speak these words, so how can I expect any less from you? That you too would become swallowed in the confusion that I exhale. But you don't see, you don't really get what I'm saying, not really because I haven't even managed to start at the start, begin at the beginning. Really, I've told you nothing so far."

But will you?

"I will…I will tell my story. I will call it Excruciate. You know what it means? Excruciate?"

I have an idea.

"It means, as a verb, 'to inflict severe pain upon; torture: to cause mental anguish; to irritate greatly.' As an adjective, it means 'extremely painful; causing intense suffering; unbearably distressing; torturing.' Shit, right? And I don't even know which of those strings of words deserves the most amount of punch. Pronouncement. It's all just so god-damn *severe*. It's torture. The anguish was unexplainable, is unexplainable. Anguish. Suffering. Distressing. And then if I were to add in my own, you know, to customize the term, to make 'Excruciate' my own, I would tell you too that it is a haunting. She haunts me still. It's not just unknown galaxies spinning madly above my skull. They are named by me and they are real and tangible, if only to me. They are born of memories and their relentless pursuit of me. These galaxies – they exist. They are the way the wind blows the first scent of autumn's approach; she is there. It's Alana Miles on FM radio running her course-silk voice over Black Velvet; she has entered the vehicle. It's a grove of trees, it's the curve in the highway, it's the ply-wood enclosed lacrosse box peeling green paint, it's the hum of the generator where we are tucked into the corner by the Zamboni doors. Yep, there she is. All these years, decades gone by, yet still she waits for me, lurks around corners for me, curls her finger and gives the coy smile that tells me I'm about to taste the perfume from her chest again; still she haunts me."

Now you are telling the end though, aren't you?

"I suppose so. The gentle version of the end. Though really, the end doesn't come. Does it?"

It could.

"It could? How could it?"

Maybe you tell it?

"Haven't I been?"

15

You've done well. But no, you haven't been. You've been playing peek-a-boo with it. Beating around the bush. Tell it now in its fullness.

"Just warming up."

Stalling.

"Hesitating."

Afraid?

"Terrified."

You find this difficult to talk about. May I make a suggestion?

"You may."

What if instead of us talking about 'it' and all that 'it' is we talk instead about an object?

"What kind of object?"

That is what you will decide. If all of what happened, any of the timelines or situations that are included to make up the whole of your experience could be given an object what would it be?

"I'm not sure. I feel confused."

Can we start with a shape? A color?

"It is black. It is shiny and black. It is an orb. From the orb, there are jagged and fragmented outcroppings."

Where does it live?

"It lives in my forehead." A touch to the third eye. "It lives in my sternum." A clutching by the right hand at the breast bone. "A place that is vivid and alive."

Does it move?

"It vibrates and swirls. It pokes at my brain and my heart."

Does it travel?

"It does."

Where does it travel?

"Out of me."

How does it get out of you?

"It swells until it rips through the flesh of me, breaching the barrier of the skin and bones and blood of me until it is exposed and pulsing and I extend into the space around me many feet in front of me."

Does it have a feeling?

"It is colder than ice and then it burns."

Chapter 2
Passage

"The beginning was 1996. I was 14. I wore yellow Stussy jeans, wide at the knees, wide all the way down. Mustard yellow. Ha. Why? Why because it's the only thing I owned that was name-brand. And a Blue sweater with the fire department logo on it. It's hard to tell even this part. I'm embarrassed for myself. Because that's the shit I had control over and I didn't even do that right."

So, I'm 14 and I'm a troubled kid. Broken home, alcoholics, and psychiatric disorders; the ugly ones. The bad ones. And I've got a dad who's dying in the Intensive Care Unit in the city over an hour away from home. And home isn't really home because I'm pretty sure that they are fucking aliens. And that's not one of the psychiatric disorders talking. I'm not one of the psychiatric disorders in the family. I used to think I must be the alien; I was so different from them. It took a long time for me to realize that it's them who are alien. Actually though, I'm not entirely convinced of that, even today, even with the rest of the world, I listen to them talk and their content baffles me. I do not understand their language that speaks of a world so much gentler than my own in so many ways, and yet there appears to be an ease in them, them – the people around me – an ease that allows humans to suggest that this is ok, this is sane. The hate and the hurt.

I just don't get it. I never have. Even for all my scars. Even for all the sharp ends of the blade I've been on, all the weapons I've shied away from as they come hurtling toward me aiming to impale me.

But back to it. It was 1996 and I wore mustard-colored gangsta' jeans. I'm walking down a hallway at the south end of the high school. That part there, about the south end, that might be the only bit of fiction I thread into this story. I'm just guessing, I don't really know if it was south or east or any which other way. I'm terrible with navigation. Except when I have the Google Maps pulled up and the British version of Siri is talking me through my next left in 650 meters.

I think someone might have spoken to Her first…I'm coming to the part in the story where I introduce you to Her. This gets me a little jumbled. Before she and I met, she was given the run-down. Maybe it was Meryl, could have been my mother. But I doubt that. Probably Meryl, maybe Rose. Meryl was my rent-a-friend. My 'street-side counselor.' Paid to play nice with the street-entrenched youth of the Valley. I'm not being disparaging. Not of her. And Rose, she was my 'substance abuse counselor.' I don't know that it's important but I'll just say that I wasn't addicted. I wasn't a junkie. I was a survivor. I did just enough drink and drug to accomplish two things. One: stay sane. Two: stay safe; do just enough, smoke just enough, snort just enough, drop and swallow just enough to keep the others from noticing that you're just not into it. Keep tough and keep them looking in another direction. Two things: stay sane and stay safe.

"Two years after the mustard yellow Stussy jeans, I was neither safe nor sane."

Tell me how you got there.

"There?"

Yes. To the place that was neither safe nor sane.

"I'll continue then. I walked down the south (maybe west) hallway heading toward a corner of the school, tucked furthest away from the mainstream traffic. A few different programs ran over in that corner: Learning Assistance, LA; that was for the few books short of an encyclopedia group…should I find a way to modernize this part? I'm not very techie. Does it make sense to say a few megabytes short of a website? Probably not but I'm impressed I even came up with that. Anyways, Learning Assistance; wasn't for me. Then there was the Special Ed room; for those more in need than the services provided in LA. That room, Special Ed, it had three doors, one from the main hallway on one side of the room and on the opposite side, a doorway leading to the wooden wheelchair ramp that leads to a long and narrow parking lot, secluded, by the rugby field.

I feel rough right now. My heart is just slamming in my throat and the left side of my neck. My knee has been bouncing for quite a few minutes now, but this part, talking about the room, getting closer, now my stomach is clenched and there is a bit of bile rising up. It's a storm inside my brain and my belly and my heart. The aching is back and I'm just plain fucking terrified that I'll remember too much and it'll hurt so bad and I'll forget again that this isn't

1996…or '97 or '98 or '99…those were bad *bad* years and I thought I'd never heal. And I thought I'd never forget."

And have you forgotten?

"I've worried I would."

But have you?

"Some parts of my body have. Some of the pain and the pleasure too, some of that doesn't live in me anymore. And I have forgotten some things. Like her birthday. I remember the girls still. I shouldn't call them 'the' girls. They are 'Her' girls. Playtime ended and we don't play house anymore. They are 'Her' kids. July 6th and April 29st. That's their birthdays. But I don't remember hers. I remember the town she came from. I remember every time I drive to my favorite close-to-home vacation spot, every time I'm two hours away from it and I see the sign announcing 'Holden.' I remember her parent's name, I think, Brian and Val…this is more that I've said in ages and I'm starting to squirm, there is a pain in my chest now and I don't have any Ativan."

What do you need?

"For it to not have happened."

But it did.

"It did."

And you remember.

"Too much."

Yet still, you worry that you are forgetting.

"Some parts."

And that's why you tell your 'story' now?

"That's why…

The Special Ed room had a third door. It led to a small office, with another door across from it and a window on the end looking out onto the back parking lot and the wooden wheelchair ramp. The door that leads to another room led to the program called 'Passage.' And that's where so much of it happened. Where the stolen touches graced my lips and my thighs. Where an angel lit upon me and brought me to worship at the altar of her groin. I found religion in that room. I found a creature to exalt and offer sacred service to. She breathed life into my drowning lungs and whispered seductions that tore angel wings from my shattered spine. That room needs an exorcist now.

I wonder if this will be the hardest part. I feel a little more resolved now. It has to be told. And you said to start at the beginning. Huh…."

What is the 'huh' for?

"It just sounded wrong, me saying to start at the beginning. It sounds so much better to say 'begin at the beginning' or 'start at the start'; the two phrases shouldn't be intermingled…"

Is this you stalling?

"It might be."

Should you?

"Should I what?"

Should you stall?

"She was the god-damned Taurus, not me! Some people can put their heads down and just bowl through things. Maybe I can't."

Is that what I suggested?

"Maybe not in so many words. But I don't think I can be rushed."

I don't mean to rush you. Direct you. I mean to direct you. That's what I'm here for, to help. From afar.

"I know. I know.

So, in the beginning, there was a room. No. In the beginning, there was an office in between two rooms. In the office, there was a gray and beige armchair on one end of the room, the end opposite the window looking out onto the back parking lot. In front of that window, there was a computer on a desk. The room was longer than it was wide; maybe three times longer. On both side walls, there were windows. The windows took up most of the walls. They looked into the two rooms that the office was between; Passage on the east and Special Ed to the west. The windows had aluminum venetian blinds on the interior. The blinds allowed for privacy. The blinds let the sad kids like me sit in the gray and beige woven armchair and cry. They let the Youth Workers who ran Passage give private counsel to the kids. They let the Youth Worker, the teacher, hold onto the crying kids like me. And those blinds let the whole universe slow down to one epic exhalation that gently blew all sense of reality away when she, we, like one being, slowly broke apart our bodies from that comforting hug, but not all the way, not enough to stop contact, just enough to allow for the weight of her arms to become like a mist, finding no friction in their movements over my body, she slid her arms from around my shoulders to my back and my waist, to hold my hands briefly and then to trail them up to my arms and to my shoulders, all of this while in fragments of millimeters, her cheek like the silk-softness of a rose grazed across my cheek, ever so slowly, stalling, halting, the edge of her lip met the corners of my mouth and like molasses on fire and then the next second cooled by a snowflake they traveled. No, we traveled together. Until her lips were upon me and her tongue-tip parted my lips and called out all of my sorrow in a silent raging scream.

A knock at the door. Yes, at that fucking second! Or seconds. I don't know how long we stayed in that alternate universe where two bodies breathed as one, heaved as one, inflamed by passion yet restful and content.

'Holy fuck. Holy fuck,' she straightened. I don't remember what I did. The blinds were closed. Holy fuck. Thank god. She unlocked the door. It was Kyle.

Kyle was another teacher. From the Native Ed class. We don't need to talk about him, do we?"

I don't know. Is he important to the story?

"No. I don't think so. I mean, he was a part of the story. I always suspected he knew. I think there were a few who knew. It's more than wondering. I am almost certain they knew; Kyle and Raphael and the lady who taught Special Ed. Not Deborah, the one who was the Teacher's Aide over there, I don't think she knew. But I also don't think she'd be surprised to hear it. But then I wouldn't be surprised if she were the first to say that I'm just a fucked-up little street kid and I'm lying. Was. *Was* just a fucked-up little street kid.

Amber, she knew. I know she knew. We talked about it. I harbor no ill feelings toward her. For knowing and not doing anything…"

What was there to do?

"The same thing Meryl did."

What did Meryl do?

"She told."

Who?

"I'm not all that certain of who all she told. She told Margaret."

And Margaret is…I'm sorry, I probably didn't need to ask. You were likely going to get there on your own. My apologies, continue please if you please.

"Margaret was the Director of the place I went to for therapy. OK, I should explain. There were different types of therapy, in layman's terms, I did group substance abuse with Rose Lane. But I shouldn't tell you the first and last names. I don't want to bring people into this. I don't want them to have to explain anything.

There was Rose and there was Meryl and there was…the one I refer to as 'Her'…should I just call her, Her?"

You should call her whatever is natural.

"Ha. Natural! What part of this haven't you heard? There is no natural here."

A second apology. And so quickly. Pardon me please, I mean no offense.

"Oh, I know. This is just getting more intense. The headache is here now. And it's so late, so early, I have to work in a couple of hours and I'm sure I won't sleep with this all still running in my head. So, I will tell you more of my story so I can exhaust the feverish worry and the person inside my head who runs on a black screen, naked, neither man nor woman, screaming and doing backflips until there is a bomb that goes off and it is palpable, it is real, and my body jolts and the figure in my mind; not even really just my mind – it is actually in my skull, it goes still and the screen stays black but now there is no frenetic energy hiding within the blackness. The blackness is still. That has happened since I was just a little kid."

Then you should call her whatever is easiest for you.

"The easiest. OK. I don't know yet. Can I really just call her, Her?"

By all means, it's your story to tell.

"To make a long story short, Meryl told Margaret."

How did Meryl know?

"I told her. OH god! I told her. I vomited for days after. Every morning when I woke up, I vomited. That lasted more than a year when every time I woke up, a dread would come upon me and I would come to know the loss all over again, fresh and sharp and cruel. Excruciate.

It was like Ground Hog Day, the movie?"

I know it.

"It was like that. No, no because this waking up, this was all and only badness. This was like Alzheimer's. This was waking up every day knowing you were crazy, knowing you were married but not knowing that your wife is dead and gone for years and having someone tell you, 'Remember Mister, remember your wife is dead?' Wailing. 'My wife is dead?!'

'How did she die?!'

'Who killed my wife, my beautiful wife, my whole-world wife, my I can't breathe without you wife?!'

It's hearing that your two children, daughters, 4 and 6, are gone. Disappeared. Dead. Vanished…ever even existed?"

When did you tell Meryl?

"I can't even recall the month, let alone the date or time. I remember where. And I remember it was daylight out. I had been playing tennis. My sister and her boyfriend attempting to have a normal interaction with my shattered self. I had a tennis racket with me. I walked to the Reconnect office, that's what Meryl's program was called, the rent-a-friend program, Reconnect. It was in the basement of the Youth Commission. Another program of some sort. Or maybe the Youth Commission was in the basement too and the sign for it was on the main floor of the building for better display. But that's not important where the sign is."

How do you decide what is and isn't important?

"I guess I'm fickle with that. Sometimes, everything seems important simply because I remember it. "

Then there is no need to edit yourself. You will add into the story any of the facts that you can recall. Then it will be told to the closest extent of its fullness.

"And then it will not be mine alone..."

It was a dark office and I liked that. There was a terracotta incense burner. It was dark and there was a couch. It had her gorgeous shawls and blankets all along with it. It smelled like patchouli and nag champa. That's what Meryl smelled like too, with a soap that I don't know mixed in with it. And menthol cigarettes for a while, and after the cigarettes Big Red gum. She would let me lay my head in her lap on that couch. She stroked my hair. She was a beautiful Mother, a Goddess, sacred for her touches that stayed in the spirit of healing me, never serving herself, always me and my innocent needs.

It wasn't on that couch; it was on a different one. Not the day of the tennis racket coming with me to Reconnect, a few days before. I realize I get the order mixed up here and there. But it's not like I can erase what I've said to

27

repeat the order once I've told it out loud. So, there was a common sitting area. Like a lounge space for youth. No one else was there. She worked when others didn't. That's when we fucked up street kids needed her. When no one else was around. I don't know what she sensed in me. Maybe I should ask her. But there must have been something. We were on a couch…the burning ice in my stomach just came back and the hammering in my throat as if my own heart attempts to choke me. This is so intense. Adjective: "extremely painful; causing intense suffering; unbearably distressing; torturing." Excruciate.

She made it a story, the type that isn't true. She let me tell her without telling her. I got to pretend it wasn't true. I don't remember what words I used, not with any exactness. But I told her the story. I told her the truth:

Maybe there is a woman that I love. Maybe she is my salvation. My Messiah. I love her with every minute aspect of myself, each finite molecule of me compiling until I am as large as the Milky Way and there is nothing minute about me or my existence anymore. We made love. We made love for years. In the school, well not all the way in the school. In the lacrosse box off of the highway by the tennis dome. In her van parked on gravel turn-offs up on Sumas Mountain, in the park by the freeway heading east toward Yarrow, Hogan Park. She lived in Yarrow for a while, not while I was with Her. In the bathrooms at the soccer field on Delair road. In the apartment on Laurel Street. That's the apartment we shared. A two-bedroom, ground-floor unit on the front side of the building. The girls had bunk beds in their room. I would tuck them in, I would say bedtime prayers, and I would kiss their foreheads and the outside of the little one's soother that was tucked securely in between pale pink cherub lips. I told her maybe she left me. I told her likely I was crazy. It made me crazy. I told her maybe I went to the house where she and her husband lived. Maybe I saw them sleeping through the window to their room off the backyard. Maybe I wanted to shoot him. Maybe I had a gun. Maybe I would kill him. Likely I'd just kill me.

Chapter 3
Searching Through Dichotomy

"I had been to their house. That was during the first months of our…what do I call it, 'Love Affair.'"

You can call it whatever it was.

"But that's the thing. It's not just a simple as begin at the beginning because I don't even know what it was. How to name an unknown. How do I define the story that I am telling? I am still imprisoned. I don't even know what happened to me! Was I loved or was I victimized? Can both exist as one? Was this a Love Affair or sexual exploitation? There are so many conflicting pieces of data. Data, see now I'm handling it like the nurse I am. But the nurse in me came much later. More than a decade later. I cannot reconcile the myriad of things that took place, each grouped into categories that seem profoundly good and alternately desperately bad. Wrong. Evil. But I don't think that was her. Not evil."

You asked, can both exist as one? That is a question you will need to answer.

"Yes, I can see that it is. And maybe in this process, I will come to know?"

The knowing is in you already. It is the process that will reveal it.

"Then for that, I am eager. I will continue…

He would go away for work. 'He' is her husband. I probably shouldn't name him. When he would go away for work, I would go over. The girls, no *Her* girls, were asleep. There was beer. Bloody disgusting but she drank beer and Clamato juice. Stomach turning. Give me clam and vodka and a good hit of Tabasco with the rest of the seasonings and I'm good. Add a little pickle juice and the taste goes to a whole new level…"

Are you veering away for a reason? What's your pulse doing? Your stomach and your head?

"It's not good. It's painful. There are levels of pain existing in my psyche that are immeasurable. I wish there was a Richter scale for this kind of shit. I feel like if it could be measured I could be vindicated. People would be forced to see the suffering she caused."

Vindication. Hm. Who do you want to know? Who do you want to see?

"Huh. I don't know entirely. The school board. The courts. The girls, they're grown now. I often wondered if they had friends, as teenagers, that she, Her, found 'special' like me."

Will you tell them – the school board, the courts…?

"Oh, the school board knows. The administrators of the high school knew. They protected her. Ha! They kicked me out! As for the courts, I talked to a lawyer once. On the phone. A human rights lawyer. Big shot, super famous in her circles. But I couldn't do it. It was so raw. I couldn't say anything without throwing up and going without sleep for days at a time, ending up in the psych ward. And I couldn't face someone hearing it all, or that which could be revealed, and telling me, 'Innocent.' Saying she hadn't done it – I'm the fucked up little lying street kid. But also, I couldn't bear to hear 'Guilty.' Guilty of what? As I said, I still don't know what it is. And back then, 15 years ago, she was still my Messiah.

I'll lose sleep over this, this silent speech as well. Though hopefully not as bad as the days on end it used to be. It is 15 years since I even tried telling this story."

*Note to self: PICK UP HERE WITH GOING FROM IHOP TO HER HOUSE. Good luck to me with sleeping tonight. Try not to dream. To dream, to scream, to come unraveled.

Chapter 4
Shattered

You seem different today.

"Different? Different, how?"

Different like 'morose.'

"Morose? Huh. I like that word. Morose. It's soft and slow. The sound of the word is like the sound that the word means. Morose. Yes. Yes, I do like that word. Like 'obese.' That's a good word too. Or, maybe not a good word but a word that sounds like the word means. Obese. Oh-bese. Bese, like 'beast.' Oh-Beast. But not a fierce beast because there isn't really anything hard about the word is there? Like 'morose,' it's a soft word. Maybe that's because of the b and the o and the s all lined up closely to each other. All curly letters except for the letter e. Oh-bese. The e really is the only bit of definition in the word and really then only if you think of it capitalized. I write in all capitals so that the way I'm envisioning it:

OBESE

Yes, really it's just that E that makes it hard. Like a hugely fat man with an erection. That one little bit of hard edge gets lost in the rest of the soft edges."

But you aren't feeling morose?

"Morose, no. But I am stoned."

You are stoned...

"I am."

OK...

"Just a little CNS depressant."

A CNS depressant...

"Yep. Central Nervous System depressant."

Yes, right, I too know that. And why are you stoned?

"Too much. Too much from last time I told my story. Got started telling my story. There was no sleep, there was vomit, there was begging for the morning so that finally, the curtains would cease their shadow play on the wall and her hair would stop flowing from the fabric, her fingertips sliding along the walls reaching toward me, seeking to drag me into the scent and touch and taste filled dreams of her. Of her angst. So I took a pill. I'm relaxed."

And you are OK to proceed?

"Am I?"

I trust you know the answer. You know if you want to tell the story.

"Right...But can we just reestablish first...this shit is real? Like, *real* real."

And how do you cope with that? With the realness?

"I thought I was doing fine. Thought it wasn't just being kept at bay – the fear, the worry, the haunting. I thought I had grown past it...they say time heals all wounds."

But you haven't...

"No, I haven't. I did good though. Played it out very well. And I'd like to think that once I'm finished telling the story, it will be emptied from me and I can leave it in another person's eardrums and I will have shed the rough leather skin, the heavy metal chain mail, the acid burned flesh and live in my own fresh pinkness of a life spent outside of her influence and memory."

And if that doesn't work?

"Oh, I imagine this all will be cathartic either way. Perhaps, it will be a full purge. I will remove the undesired from Her powerful position inside the core of me."

So she is undesired?

"I think we were talking about something else before this weren't we?"

We were.

"What was it?"

I think what matters is what you want to talk about now.

"I want to talk about what we said we would talk about last time."

Last time you were telling me about what you wanted to tell to who. I think it is important though that we come back to this statement that claims Her as the undesired.

"Perhaps we will. Come back to it…"

For now, we can carry on where it is that you want to go. You left a message for yourself when we last finished. Do you remember it?

"I'm thinking. I'm thinking back to what we said. To what I said. To what I told. What I told you and told Meryl and what I ended up telling Margaret and eventually what I told the police. And that, that part with the police, that wasn't much. That was a lie. That was me protecting the sanctity of my god. I would never have let them take her away. And leave the girls, those beautiful girls. They were so young and perfect and little and…no. No. No. NO. They are not *the* girls. They are *her* girls. They are adults now.

And I would indeed have been, they would have been, we would have been heartsick to have lost her but they are her girls and this did happen and we did make love and playhouse and make vows and paint our dreams and it was the only thing that felt real and it was the largest god damn illusion that ever was created. And I remember my message, I said: PICK UP HERE WITH GOING FROM IHOP TO HER HOUSE…"

You want to start from there now.

"It's one of the things I remember. It seemed so normal for anyone looking in. The IHOP off the main drag, a table of people, different ages. Me, my mother, and someone else I don't remember. One of mother's friends I expect. And the waitress, Julie. Long blond hair and beautiful, a warm smile. She was older than me but that didn't take much, I was fifteen. So looking back now, I'd say she was early to mid-twenties. I don't know if I had a cell phone with me, no I didn't. I must have used the payphone in the vestibule of the restaurant. It must have been a pre-planned call. Well, at some point we spoke, Her and me. And the all-clear was given, the kids are asleep. The husband is gone. Julie drove. It was after her shift and I don't know where my mother thought I was going. I should ask. I've thought of asking other people what they saw/heard/thought/felt but I'm so afraid to get caught up in it. Dragged into them and their experience making my own experience become either too much more real or becomes less-than because it was shared."

Judy dropped me off on the opposite side of the street and a few houses down. My heart is hammering in the side of my neck like a Tyco drum; if I put my fingers to the carotid, it is bouncing my finger like a trampoline. That's what's happening right now I mean. Though it probably happened then too.

It was my first time at her house. She met me at the bottom of the stairs. I'm glad she was just wearing regular clothes and didn't open up to me in a black fucking lingerie or anything; that would have been too much like tawdry daytime television. I think I would have been disgusted. Because do remember, I...whoa wait a minute! 'Do remember,' I said. How the hell can you 'do remember' I haven't even told you so how could you possibly remember? Funny that. I have these sensations with you. Subtle, oddities that I cannot name come up when I sit across from you, your face mildly obscured. I recognize you, but you can seem so undefined...

You were saying – 'do remember' what?

"Not 'do remember.' Do *know*, that for me, she was all purity. This was not a love affair, or a crime, or adultery. This was the truest and purest of love. It defied what was accepted – we were that blessed! So said my child mind."

And so she didn't open her door in lingerie.

"No. But I don't know now what she was wearing. I could see the landing of the main floor, lightly lit, from a kitchen light beyond my view. There was a pony wall rising up from the stairs and that went into the living room at the front left. To the right were the bedrooms and bathroom. And straight through: the kitchen to the sliding double doors and into the yard. We didn't go there. We started downstairs. Past the stairway to the left was the entrance into the above-ground basement family room/rec room. And there was an office desk on the right wall of that room.

That was Jim's. That's her husband. Straight ahead was the large TV, turned off. And along the wall to the left of our entrance was a couch; it was either a sectional couch or two couches against each other because the seating also went under the large window that faced the street. The kid's toys were in the far right corner of the room. Cozy, pretty, and clean. And I felt vaguely like an intruder. But only because of Jim's desk. When really, I realized with my second glance at it – he was the intruder.

She sat on the arm of the couch, close to the door. That's where we kissed for the first time in her house. Plenty of other times. But not so often to have not been the most sensational experience. In a foreign land: this living room of her husbands, I was kissing his wife. With my hands cupped to her breasts. I needed air. Later, I wanted to scream it at him, 'I've had your wife you mother fucker.' I can feel the visceral rage still.

We went upstairs; 'quietly' she whispered. She led me down the hall to the bedrooms, past her and her husbands. To the right; this is Ter…wait. I shouldn't say their names. Not the girls. Not Her girl's names. I've wondered about the other names and worried that I shouldn't use them. Actually, this is the first time I've used His name, the husband's name in 18 years. But Her girls? No, I know I shouldn't use theirs."

That's good. Trust yourself in this process.

"So to the right, she whispered, 'this is so-and-so's room,' and we peek in and I'm seeing her impeccable red lips that are so slight but filled with plump vibrancy, so much like her mothers. She really does look just like her – even today. I've seen them. Not today, but a few years ago

38

now, only as images on a computer. And then to the left, here is the 'other so-and-so's room.' This was the youngest so-and-so. The youngest girl, two at the time. And she didn't have her blankets on and her leg was hanging off the bed and there was another mattress or some padding or something like that on the floor right by the bed. And she had a soosy in her mouth; that's a soother.

But maybe I've got them reversed and really it was the youngest on the right and the eldest on the left and really it was Tes…almost did it again, used one of their names. And maybe it was really the eldest who slept out of the blanket. I'm just not sure about all of that and that gets me so worried because where did the memories go and will they ever return and will all of the others follow? And it's not the amnesia of it all that frightens me, that distresses me, because like I said I would like for all of this not to have happened and so, one might say that isn't forgetting the best thing that could happen? But I need them to understand that one day, if my memories are all gone, the fright is that in old age, I will still suffer under Her and no one will know what I suffer from. So then, no one will be able to help me and then – god help me – they won't know what CNS depressant to give me to help me cope, so I will just be Her victim until the day I die."

You called yourself a victim. Is that what you are?

"You fucking tell me! I don't know what I am or what I was or where I will go and become and think and feel in any way what-so-bloody ever when it comes to her, will I?!"

I think you might.

"Oh 'might' I? …You see it's not fair, me hollering at you and it's not your fault. None at all, your fault. But I've got to yell at someone don't I? And who could that be? But by the way how could it help to yell and holler and roll my eyes, scoffing…it won't that's what."

So who will you yell at?

"No one. Well, that's a lie. I will yell. I'll yell at whoever is close when the confusion and fear and loathing and longing and passion and pain – the excruciate – comes too close to the surface of my psyche to cope with and so I summon my sorrows and spit them out as rage. That's what I do now. That's how I love and that's how I lose love. Because if you scratch the surface too deeply, scratch it at all, and I learn that I'm not healed, I'm not ok, this is not resolved and sanity slips away."

But the yelling doesn't help?

"No. Not in the long run. But in the minute, the minutes, the moment? Oh! I love the feel of the bass vibrating out of my chest and into my throat and I can feel my veins warm with the rush of it and my eyes become sharper, more focused. And the stillness that follows the release is the most serenity I have known since I was ripped from the breast of a beloved."

And so that's why you are here?

"Yes, that's why I'm here. I'm here because the yelling doesn't help and the pretending to forget doesn't help and the drinking doesn't help and the cigarette that I picked up four months ago doesn't help and not acknowledging that I needed help back then doesn't help. I'm just not doing as good of a job at pretending to be normal anymore. And I think people are about to discover that I am a fraud."

A fraud? How do you mean?

"I am not what I appear. I am not the all-together-totally-with-it educator/nurse/facilitator/teacher that I seem to be. I am a wreck; mangled steel and shrill screaming voice, blood leaking along the freeway and into the gutter in a black river that glints red in the shine of the headlights of the passersby; too busy to stop, to look, to staunch the bleeding."

Then again, maybe you are.

"Are what?"

Maybe you are all together. Totally with it.

"Explain."

Maybe you get to have both. Be both. What if you had this experience and you also have every experience that comes after it as well. Just the same as all that happened before Her remains intact. Maybe you are both; at one time shattered and now all together, 'with it.' Maybe you remember being shattered but you yourself are not shattered.

"I don't know that I can see it that way."

Imagine yourself in front of a mirror.

"OK."

It's a full-length mirror, right?

"Making adjustments. Yes, now it is full length. It was an oval with a thick border, wrong word, a thick frame. It was ornate, carved with filigree and shit like that. Anyways, it's full length now. Boring, plain black frame on a narrow rectangle. Don't want to see too much of my width at once! Ha."

Either way. The mirror doesn't much matter. Not for this imaging and not for the ways of how it shows beauty. See the mirror.

"Yes."

See yourself.

"Yes."

The physical self.

"Yes."

Your head and your face.

"Yes."

Your brown eyes.

"With a hint of orange sometimes, yes."

Your shoulders.

"Tattooed."

Your arms.

"Also tattooed."

Your hands.

"Yes."

Your chest…

"Also tattooed."

Your chest leading to your stomach.

"Soft."

Your thighs and your legs – I'll beat you to it – strong, defined. Your feet, on the ground.

"Yes."

Are you solid?

"Yes."

Are you whole?

"Yes."

That cup in your hand?

"Whiskey. Yes?"

Throw it at the mirror.

"Huh. What?!"

Throw it at the mirror.

"You won't mind the mess?"

I won't mind. Throw it.

"Arrrgh!"

"Yes, I did."

Is the mirror broken?

"Yes."

Step away from the mirror. Turn your back on the cracks and fissures and chunks carved out.

"Yes."

Look at the ground. Are your feet on it?

"Yes."

Look at your legs. Are they missing any mass?

"No."

Look at your hands and your arms and your torso. And they bleeding, broken, bruised? Are they absent any parts?

"No."

Look back. Is the mirror shattered?

"Yes."

Are you shattered? Don't look at the mirror, it will tell you what to see.

"What?"

Don't look into the mirror. The reflection is wrong. She broke the reflection. She breaks the reflection still. Don't look in the mirror, it will tell you what to see. Instead, tell us, tell me, what to see.

Chapter 5
A Pink Freckle and Bile

"We ended up in the backyard. There wasn't a porch. Not like the porch I want to have on my house one day. Wooden planks that span the back wall of the house, will echo the footsteps of dogs and children and friends into the cold black soil that runs rich beneath the boards. Hers was a concrete slab. It felt good on my feet, cold. There was a row of tall, old cedars, or cypress hedges I think. They ran about 16 feet from the back wall of the house, a view of them from the kitchen window. A weird spot for hedges I always thought because it blocks the view of so much of the yard. But maybe, a part of this is muddled in the vision of my memory. Maybe they were further, maybe they were nearer. But either way, I remember a row of them along one section of the yard, not taking the entire width of the yard, but leaving an opening. There was a trampoline. But it was dark and maybe it was the circle of a pool and not a trampoline. Likely it's negligible. I just want to tell it all."

I didn't go into the yard. We stayed on the concrete patio. She sat on the step. She smoked a cigarette. I loved the way she looked. There was kind of a mole...mole sounds ugly. There was kind of a pretty freckle above and beside her top lip. It was pink, not brown like other freckles. I liked the shape of her lip when she puffed on the white filter with the green pinstripe line wrapped above it. I liked what that shape of her lip did to the pink freckle. She had a beer with Clamato. God, disgusting. Funny, I think the only thing left to say about this night in particular, this first time of being at her home, in Her house, seeing Her girls asleep in their beds, kissing another man's wife is that on the left side of her house, from my angle, that night which was with my back to the yard, looking down at Her smoking, is that there is a line of cedar hedges and a concrete walk with a few steps. I took a few steps over that way, past the bathroom and their bedroom windows and puked up my IHOP fries and gravy.

She pulled out the garden hose, later than 1 o'clock that morning, and hosed it down 'so Jim doesn't see when he comes home in the morning.' I don't know who picked me up that night, or if anyone did. I don't know where I went or where I lived. I only know that saying all of that brought the bile back up my throat.

Chapter 6
The Rapist

You told me I was going to meet Her. I haven't yet.

"Maybe it was the first day at the high school – Go Lions! – the day that I wore the mustard yellow. Whoa. And holy! I just remember they would tease me, they being the Passage staff, a friendly teasing, 'you've got style, you've got grace, you've got mustard on your face, you're a weeeinner.' Whoa."

That first day she asked me if I was a lesbian. Haha! Now here's where the story gets a little trickier. But I don't want you to get lost in this next part. It's too much for some people. It bogs them down, this little piece of information. So I'll explain that bit about the lesbian a little later, just keep thinking of me as you had been. Likely, that's going to come closest to the truth anyway.

So, 'are you a lesbian?' she asks me. I held Her gaze, turned my eyes to a hard slant, 'And who the fuck are you to know?' I said in response and walked away. What is it with therapists, that's a huge part of what she was as a 'Youth Worker,' a therapist. What is with them thinking that they can be privy to people's deepest and darkest and all that shit? And right off the get-go? Is it written in the pre-reqs to the program entrance – must be egotistical and have a hero complex?

We didn't have a conversation again for a few days, Her and I. She told me later that really impressed her, my 'who the fuck are you to know' comment. She liked my attitude. Ha! And Ha! again because you know what 'therapist' actually spells right?

Tell me.

"Spell it out for yourself."

I know the spelling – T.H.E.R.A.P.I.S.T.

"Great. Smart. Now I'll spell it. T.H.E R.A.P.I.S.T."

I see. Is that what she is? The Rapist?

"I can't tell."

Chapter 7
Crying God's Name

"Meryl took me for long drives in her sun-bleached-blue pretty-much-faded-to-a-shade-of-gray one greater than white station wagon. She smoked menthols and I would bum a few sometimes. She sang to me. Different songs, most I hadn't heard before. Probably, all of them I hadn't heard before but looking back now, they are familiar, but only because of her, and that's why I thought I knew them all along. There is one I sing still. I don't know all the words and I don't know how it's sung; I just sing it my way:

> *All babies are born crying god's name*
> *Over and over all born crying god's name*
> *God gives them the stars to use as a ladder*
> *Over and over all born crying god's name*

They might not even be the right words but that's what I sing. I spoke with Meryl recently. I mentioned the song to her. She tells me it is by Sinead O'Connor."

Is this a part of your story? Or is this the indication that you are done for now?

"Um. Done? No, not done. Yes, I think it's a part of the story. I think I've kind of separated them now. Her and Meryl. But they used to be so intertwined I couldn't speak of her, Meryl, either. Not without the touches of melancholy sorrow coming and settling upon me for days on end. They are not synonymous, Her and Meryl, but the story wraps Meryl up in it the way she wrapped me in her cloaks and her patchouli. I often wished she would brew a spell for me and cast Her out. I don't know if it's OK to out Meryl as a witch. I'll hope she doesn't mind. Or, I hope that you will forget."

I'm here to help you remember what you can and to draw up that which you can't recall just yet. I'll forget if you tell me to.

"How about a joke? A little comedic relief. It's how I functioned so often in therapy before. 'Look for the humor,' I'd say. Here's the joke, not a knock-knock or anything. A one-liner:

Develop a taste for religion. Lick a witch.

Ha! Just the smallest bit dirty…not the witch! Ha! The joke, the joke is a small bit dirty."

Comic relief. Find the humor. I can appreciate that angle. Does this band-aide the story though? Is this how it went untold for so long? Two decades?

"It ended when I was 17, so that's 19 years gone by. But that's the end and I'm not there yet."

I suppose I'm telling you about Meryl because I ought to tell you about Maggie because she is one of the ones, the five ones, which knew any of this story of Her at all. And she doesn't know much. No one person does. They each get a fragment. A little sliver, or a small chunk, different sizes they each hold but none holding much at all, of the mirror that's broke.

My brother Marcus knew about Her. In that, I mean he knew I wrote a poem about this great love, this great secret…he stole that poem to give to a girl. He got the girl.

I had been at Her apartment, not living with her yet. It had only been a few days since she was in there and the girls needed time to adjust to not living with their daddy anymore. Fair enough. Definitely, Her girls. So either they were sleeping or they were with him. The arrangement became that he would have them for one week, then Her would have them for one week, alternating back and forth, sharing holidays.

I might as well Segway into that part now. She left him. Sonuvabitch she left him for me! She fucking left him for me because we were in fucking love and this was real and pure and true and the world couldn't stop us. Well, they could, actually. So we were going to tell them one year after I graduated, we would tell them three months after my last year of school ended that we 'now' live together but we would keep them whispering for the full year and then break the good news. Right now, it feels weird saying that she left him for me. I don't feel like me. Or I don't feel like the 'me' did back then. But of course, I don't! And that's not really what I'm trying to say anyway. You must recognize that this is hard to articulate?

I do see that. And you are doing well. I'm hearing the story, I'm sensing the bigger picture and you can feel free to spin it out the way that it unfolds as dictated by your internal process, otherwise called your inherent knowledge.

"It feels like I'm making this too messy. Like I'm bouncing around."

It's nothing that can't be followed. It's the straight road that is closer to two distances, but that doesn't mean it's the better traveled.

"OK. Thank you. I get worried, I get tired, I get anxious, I get exhausted, I get distressed, I shut down. Each step is essentially the same but exponentially harder than the one that came before."

That reminds me of something.

"It does?"

Yes. Excruciate. To suffer, to distress, to be inordinately burdened. You are telling your story.

"And I must..."

So she left him and moved into the apartment on Laurel Street. I didn't stay there all of the time because of the girls. One of the times that I did, I don't know what came over me afterward, but there was a night that I wasn't there, and I was with my brother. There must have been a bit of Southern Comfort, which I don't touch anymore. Memories of Her each time I do. And I told him *just* enough. Just enough to keep me from bursting with the dichotomy of bliss and bereavement. With Her and happy, fulfilled, entire, complete, serene, free; and waiting for my turn to be with her again, bereft.

And as soon as I said that 'waiting for my turn to be with her,' just now, I saw John Tommy. Another kid who hung around Her at school. It was about a year after she left that I thought of him. Of him with Her. And it just smacked me in the face right now and then rammed me in the gut so hard that I lost my breath. Literally lost it.

But right now, I'm telling you about Marcus and how days later in school, days after the night of Southern Comfort, she was in line in the cafeteria and now I can't remember which one of them it was that always got the curly fries but she was in line and either Marcus or Her was getting curly fries and Marcus came up behind her and whispered, 'so how was Crash'? She couldn't have been calm when she found me an hour or so later but she looked calm enough. I don't know, maybe she had had practice at this, the hiding, the cover-ups, the sneaking about. I had told Marcus that I watched Crash, this almost-porn back in that day, 18A, about a group of people that get off on being in car wrecks together. Like that's the hottest fucking thing – driving fast cars and turning over in a ditch and fucking each other's lights out with a gash on your forehead and a fractured ankle thrown up on the dash to take it deep. Holy. What the hell are people thinking? More importantly, what was I thinking telling Marcus anything at all?

Why did you tell him?

"Marcus is almost as hard to explain as she is. Actually, I could explain him anyway and you'd just have to take my word for it. I figure at some point a Creator looked into a crystal ball and saw this day put before me. And that lovely thing said to itself: 'I have got to help. That kid can't get through what's coming with the little-big heart it's got. That's not enough to get through it.' And so the Creator gave me my brother. Our hearts beat the same. And so I told him."

How did that feel?

"No clue. Can't recall the outcome. But what I do know is that it wasn't much after that She dropped me off at the bottom of the long driveway to my home and said, 'you can't stay here. She's too smart.' 'She' is Maggie. Maggie was too smart. Maggie was a threat to our existence. And it's true, I see it looking back. Maggie is so keen and intuitive and her love for me is the real mother kind, so she would have seen it. And because Maggie is not just good and not just smart. She is also powerful and in control of herself and her own; she would have not just seen us for what we were – she would have stamped us out. So I left."

No big deal though, right? Kids leave home all the time. True, that is. But when I left Maggie's home, I had nowhere to go, because Maggie was my foster mum.

There is more breadth and depth.

"It's not that significant. I had a mother and I had a father. My father was a sperm donor."

So you never knew your father?

"Oh, not a literal sperm donor, that's just how I refer to him after the abuse and abandonment. So, they did their thing and created me, the genetic disaster, and then along came my real dad, when I was six, or turning six. Right around there anyways."

A step-father.

"To outsiders, they would call him a step-father. But, no. To me, he is my father. My dad. My friend. My hero. When I cry for him, I cry for his pain at the end…and as a grown man myself now, I cry for him and the pain he must have endured as a man. As a father to his children that I don't know, to me, his child, to the women he loved. And I cry, in a keening wail, for the pain he would have stopped if he had been with us just a little longer. It wouldn't have happened, SHE wouldn't have happened and I wouldn't be fucked like I am because I wouldn't have needed a savior. And my children would have grown to know their grandad and my sister's children would have felt his love and strength and truth and they would have been sheltered from the world of having an orphaned mum."

You say she was your savior. You've referred to it a few times now – savior, messiah, god. And yet you say you were 'fucked.'

"Do I contradict myself? Very well, I contradict myself. I am Man, I am convoluted…Walt Whitman. Or something like that.

I don't know what she was because maybe like me, she was and is many things. But I do not…I. Do. Not. Want. To. Get. My. Self. Wrapped. Up. In. That! Fuck! This isn't about what may or may not have happened to her/for her/in her or around her. This. Is. What. Happened. To. Me."

Third time the charm. I apologize. That's three apologies. And I didn't mean to insinuate that you need to explain. I was simply pointing out an observation. Thinking perhaps you would be able to draw on it to direct your course.

"And I believe I have."

*Note to self: PICK UP HERE WITH EXPLAINING LIVING SITUATION…then to bunk beds in basement suite. The last slug of my boozy drink – that with the leftover chill pills and I hope I fucking sleep tonight. No dreams. Please.

Chapter 8
Dog Piss and Flying CDs

"The smell of dog piss on carpet steaming into the atmosphere on a hot day, permeating the air throughout the entire house. That's the smell of childhood on Redwood Avenue. The one with my mother. And just now, as soon as I acknowledge that smell and that place I can see the metal tubular frame of the red bunkbeds; double on the bottom, single on the top. It barely fits the room. The door just closes to lock it in. That's my bedroom. That was my bedroom. The furnace room. No flooring, just the cement spreading from the 60 square foot floor and up the walls halfway until it reached the border that took the concrete to drywall.

Now, don't go feeling sorry for me. I liked that room. I liked that room the same way that I liked the small walk-in closet in my parents' bedroom when I was a toddler. Then my bed was the brown vinyl-covered Electrolux vacuum cleaner box. An adventure. And besides, that furnace room was furthest from the others and I needed that privacy. I'd pull the twenty-foot telephone cord to its maximum stretch and close the door behind me. There were whispered conversations in that room. There was a coy voice on her end telling me the most outrageously beautiful things about my body. There was laughter and there was sorrow, the sweetest type of sorrow; the one that is the pining for a love that I knew would be realized in mere hours, while the night sky painted itself from black to indigo and dawn was approaching and she told me where her hands were on her body and her voice was sleepy and slippery and hushed and ragged. When I was locked in that furnace room and Her husband was away.

That room was in the basement of my father's house. He was dead by then. I think about that house and I think about Her standing at the basement door, through the garage. And I see at the same time the bucket of clams that we dug from the charcoal gray grit in Point Roberts; they sat too long in the back of the truck, me and my sister and the clams under the fiberglass canopy bumping along home. What strikes odd to me is that the day the clams died was years before she stood at the door.

It smelled like piss because we rented the upstairs to a couple that ended up being first off, fantastic potheads that cooked up the most delicious honey hash. But they lost their shit and went to crack and eventually, their three dogs, Rottweilers and a Pitty, ran the place and turned it into one big puppy-piss-pad.

Even before the living-room-sized puppy-piss-pad, there was a scent of piss tied to that house.

We had dogs as a child. Muffy, Bootsie, and PJ. And more I'm sure. There was a little orange one; I feel like I knew his name just a month ago, but that piece of my past seems to have faded to non-existence too.

Buddy!

His name was Buddy and my father, the sperm-donor one, kicked him across the room and into the fireplace. Unlit. As if that really makes it any better. If I'd have said 'he kicked him into the wall' you would not have said, 'phewf, at least the wall wasn't on fire.'

So Buddy was kicked into the fireplace and Muffy was run over by a car in our front yard when I was supposed to be inside doing homework while my mother and dad were out. But instead, I was rollerblading and shooting a squished-flat beer can between two sticks propped against the concrete barriers that lined the corner of the road that wrapped near the front of our property. Muffy was asleep on the front yard one minute and then screaming and dragging the back end of her body in circles all along the roadway, guts, and blood dripping, splashing and spurting out of her. And I couldn't do anything but stand back dumb-faced, crying, watching her and trying not to watch her, running to her and then once close running away from her. Torn between two horrors; watching her suffer and die from a distance or watching her suffer and die with my hands on her...but I didn't know what death was and I was all alone and I was only nine. And that was my dog. I dressed her up in doll clothes and pushed her around in a stroller for most of her life. That was my dog. And the woman that hit her drove away; leaving us both on the road, crying and dying."

I wonder what the neighbors thought of our house. I wonder what they whispered when we shared the road with them. I wonder who it was that always called the cops. And were they irritated and just wanted to shut the screaming woman up – my mother – or did they hope that maybe someone would come and help us all? Did they do it for compassion? Did they laugh at us? Roll their eyes at us? Did they grieve just a little, from a distance, for us? The echoing crash of smashing dishes; too dirty! my mother would scream. The CDs being flung like alien saucers, shining multi-colored dream coats into the sky from our bedroom windows; 'clean your room, look at this mess!' my mother would shrill. Dresser drawers ripped from the bureaus and tossed in the air to land as a maddened decoration in the distorted landscape of our house. The dog pissed. 'The dog pissed on the fucking floor,' she would say and her teeth were grit and when released, she did this fucked-up thing, that turns my stomach still, of folding her tongue under itself and then chomping down on it and white pus-like spittle would congeal at the corners of her mouth and she would rub our noses into the wet carpet screaming, 'smell it, smell it, can't you smell that fucking filth.'

So it wasn't just the crack heads. The living-room-puppy-piss pad was ours long before.

"So that furnace room was a sanctuary and that phone line, all twenty feet, a lifeline. I went to that from Maggie's. From the home that gave me love and peace and all the emotional and physical feeding I needed to nourish my sick soul. I went from there because 'she's too smart.' I had to protect my divine love – I hope you can hear my bitter fucking sarcasm when I say that."

I can. And that's important for you, that I hear your sarcasm?

"I don't know what is important to me right now. I'm just expressing what I can and I'm not confident that I can do that much right. But ya, I guess you are hearing my

58

bitterness, in recognizing my sarcasm, I cannot bear to feel as foolish as I do for really believing that She was divine."

You want me to think of her as neither good nor bad, to just allow the perception of Her to change as it does within you?

"Yes. It's a wonder you know that…"

You left the sanctuary of Maggie's…

"I went back to my mother's because I'd move in with Her soon enough. And we would tell everyone one year after I had graduated that we were together, in love. And we would be a beautiful happy family. The four of us and one more child together, a girl to match the other girls, and all of their names would end up rhyming. After my dad."

Does this bring you to the middle of the story then? It feels like we have progressed past what felt like the introductory parts.

"I have, haven't I?"

It seems that way.

"But I shouldn't have. No, I'm not done with the start. I will back up.

I would go to the Passage room instead of regular classes. The recommendation from the school I went in to grade eight, that invited me not to come back, had told this school administration that I'd need anger management and intensive emotional support along with behavior modification for the safety of others. I'd swing punches and I'd throw fists but never once did I hurt someone who wasn't gunning for me. Nor would I hurt someone weaker; I was the bully of bullies, and I'm not ashamed of that. They tried to shame me though, the administrators. The man who ran Passage, Raphael Frank, told me after the first year the message that he received from my grade eight year was that I would not graduate high school and I wouldn't accomplish anything in life that would bring a benefit to society. Yep, they were right. I didn't finish high school. I didn't finish high school because I was fucking my teacher-therapist and too busy dealing with the fall out of that to focus one iota on something as insignificant as x equals y and a verb is an action word and let me tell you: the things I learned on the street are more pertinent to anything in philosophy or psychology and the things I learned under sweaty bedsheets was more religion than a theology class – I never needed those classes, they couldn't have taught me a scrap of what I wasn't already learning.

I know. People don't get it. You don't even get it."

I might surprise you.

"Yes. I'm sure. With your book smarts. Thick-rimmed geek glasses and a mahogany desk make you highly intellectual don't they?"

Is this about intellect?

"It was sarcasm."

I hear that. Is this about intellect?

"No, it's not about intellect. It's about a common experience. There is no way that I can make words turn this language of my foreign experience into something that you can relate to. Something you can get."

So it's not about intellect. Again, I might surprise you.

"I would go to Passage and I would ha, 'study' for a while. She had her desk by the rear door. Like the room next door, it had a window looking into the back parking lot and there was a wooden ramp leading to the door. The side of her desk was against that window and the front of it pushed against the wall, that had the window, that looked into the office. A lot of windows, a lot of doors; a lot of opportunity for people to catch a glimpse of what was…what was what? What was 'happening'? What was 'occurring'? What we were doing…she was doing? There were a lot of windows and I know there were indeed glimpses. A woman named Ann, was an assistant next door in Special Ed. I think she saw us kiss once. I looked up at one point in our embracing, I saw a shocked look – her face white and jaw slack – and she was backing away from the windows. But she never said a thing. Actually, she may have, but it didn't amount to anything more.

And Raphael – have I explained he was Her boss?"

You hadn't, but this will qualify it.

"Raphael did what he didn't normally do. And Raphael was a man of habit. No, not of habit. Habit intonates a lack of forethought – Raphael was pure precision, he was thoughtful of each movement and he did things with intention. So when he did what he normally didn't do – it was a sign that he was thinking, he was considering, he was being strategic. He one day, not long after I think Ann saw us kiss, stood on the Special Ed side of the office. Just beforehand, he had been in the office, alone. The venetian blinds on the set of windows, those furthest from the chair and closest to the window that looked from the Special Ed room in, were open. That never happened. And there Raphael stood, hands in the pockets of his Dockers, in a stance that looked too much like an attempt at nonchalance, in a three-quarter profile to us in the office looking out at the parking lot. It was a message we both read clear, Her and I, he was watching."

Chapter 9
Soul Fucked

"I bade the beast to sleep, but it seems Her slumber is incomplete. There has been a distant grumbling – long-time rolling like the thunder clouds that track the prairie skies. She grows now. And Her presence leads me to a soul-fucked groaning. That's what I am."

You are what?

"A soul-fucked groaning. I do not simply groan; I am the groaning. This is not a head-fuck."

Then it is what?

"This is not merely a mind invaded by sorrow, the absence of reality with the façade of normality, or worse still and truer to my experience – the real having been distorted to a degree that paints it unbelievable. No, not a head-fuck. It's a god-damned calamity on my soul. She left me soul-fucked. And how do I heal from there? And if my slumber were no longer a slave to her and my subconscious could be free of Her…"

Then what?

"Then what? Then what? Why care to address the 'then' when I know that to purge her from my thoughts would be to carve out a section of my soul so that I might be beautifully incomplete without Her? I was so young. She was woven into my center and she decided the trajectory of my growth. That's one of the things I am ashamed of."

Why are you ashamed?

"For the amount I suffer."

Your suffering is shameful. How is that so?

"What I am telling you is every fourteen-year-old boy's wet dream. I fucked a cougar. I got laid every day while other kids my age were beating off on Blossom and Saved by the Bell…that is not really my humor, that vulgarity. That is me playing at un-affected. Because I am supposed to be aren't I? Unaffected?"

I'm not convinced that you are.

"I am the un-raped rape victim. And maybe John Tommy was too…"

You mentioned him earlier.

"The day she left Jim, she came to me in class. English. We were studying Of Mice and Men but I had read it so many times already that I had a book in my lap, tucked under the desk, and I was reading that instead, Look Homeward Angel by Thomas Wolfe. She slipped me a note. Her lips touched my ear as she whispered into it. Her breast grazed across my arm. She put the note in my hand on my lap and danced her fingers along my thigh. I read it. In curly penciled printing, 'I did it. I left him.' And as I looked up to meet her eyes to show her the happiness of my soul, she said, 'I have to go tell John.' She was gone from the room. I was confused – but not confused enough. I didn't know well enough to feel jealous or betrayed or suspicious. I couldn't afford to feel that. I let it roll over me and beyond me and out of reach. An hour later, we crossed in the hall.

'I'll take you anywhere you want to go. Let's just leave here.' And so we did. Down Guilford and on to South Fraser Way and pointed south to the border crossing. We joked about that. 'Let's just go – cross the line and disappear.' As if what we had here would be any less criticized and vilified there. But it was 1996 and there was Mary Kay Letourneau and we were living in another world. A fantasy.

We didn't go south, we turned left and headed up Delair road and to the park. There are two sections to the park. Perhaps I should say there 'were' two sections? A lot of time has passed now and there is likely to be more to it today. But there were two sections. At the corner, where Delair meets Old Yale road, there are ball diamonds and soccer pitches. And at the parking lot, there is a piece of green and year-round washrooms. We often went there. Once we were in the large stall, the handicapped one, first and straight ahead when you walk in the door. The city service worker came in while my hands were in her pants. We waited a few quiet moments and when we realized that the city worker would be there longer than we could, we nonchalantly zipped ourselves back up and walked out of the stall. She acted as though he had been in there assisting me. She told me, 'pretend you are handicapped.' So I put on a silent show and prayed that the person would not notice our presence and the oddity of two people sharing a stall.

We had time limits you see. Her boss, Raphael, would be waiting for us. Each 'therapeutic' excursion had time frames – there were other students that needed her time.

We would also frequent the park off of the freeway, headed toward Yarrow as well. Just off of South Parallel road was a rest stop, go past that a little way south and you come to Hogan Park. There are bathrooms there also. But even better than the bathrooms, there were large trees that allowed us to sneak kisses behind – me the fourteen-year-old with a bad past and Her, the thirty two-year-old Youth Worker.

We were caught there once too. She had picked me up one night, I think from my mother's house. I think it was the same time that she stood at the door to the basement that leads in from the garage where years before, the clams sat dead and rotting the metal bucket. We went to Hogan Park but the gates were closed. We backed out of the driveway and found a little pull-in. Again, our hands were all over each other but our pants were up. The RCMP pulled in behind us. About 10:45 at night, there was no time to do up our zippers and buttons, so we pulled our shirts down and covered our laps with our hands. It's a good thing he didn't ask her to step out of the vehicle. She wore blue jeans and a black long-sleeved shirt that tucked into the waist and was cinched into place by her black leather belt with the silver buckle. Had she needed to stand before him, he would have seen her belt and heard the jingle of the metal, he may then have been inclined to ask more questions rather than accept her explanation of needing a little time to just sit, relax, and chit chat with the kid."

Chapter 10
She Left?

"It doesn't make sense to say that she left me. That makes it seem so normal. Lovers come and go, people move on, they out-grow, they grow tired, they let go. When I say that she left me, I am ranked with millions, billions of others, and my experience becomes a part of the greater human experience."

And you don't want to be ranked in with the billions of others?

"No. Because then that is just another lie."

What comes the closest to the truth?

"What will I say instead? Instead of 'she left me' will I say she abandoned me? Will I say that she came home smelling of him and telling me she was going back to him? That I wasn't as strong and independent as she thought I was? And even that, doesn't it sound so normal, so mundane to you?"

What matters is how it sounds to you. Does it reflect your experience, your reality?

"Ha. It does not."

What does sound right to you? If I ask you what happened, what will you say?

"I will say...I will say that I was a child and that I remember this as an adult. But there is a tiny person left inside of me that has been sleeping. The dreams it had were dreadful and so it began writhing. The child murmured and sighed. It inhaled rapidly and exhaled jagged cries of pain. And so in compassion, I had to wake it, the babe that slept. I had to coax it back from the periphery of nonexistence, so that it could relate its dreams and the visions it held before the man in me took over and banished it forever to its place in the past.

What happened is that a child fell in love with a woman sixteen years older. And that woman was a mother of two and a wife to a man who closed the bathroom door in the hallway to their home, held her backward against a towel rack and raped her while her children played beyond the hollow pressboard door. That woman was a therapist. Therapist.

You are toeing the line again. You are almost giving voice to what occurred. Will you cross it?

'What's on the other side?' A quiver in my throat. A black expanse that covers me with cold sweat. An ancient void that will vacuum me in.

Perhaps that which you seek is on the other side. Perhaps, an expression of truth that will release you.

'But I wonder what that will feel like. To speak aloud and give definition to an existence that is so muddied in anti-reality. And it is only in a state of bitterness that I can claim the pain of the victim.'

And when it is not born of bitterness, what is the pain then?

67

'It is a deep and soulful sorrow. It is a grieving for a life that was meant to be elevated to freedom and peace, to Valhalla. It is an absence of fear and an attachment to a love that surpassed all expressions of love that I had known.'

In these moments, the sorrowful times, what then do you claim as the interpretation of events?

After that first kiss in the office between the two classrooms we spoke of a love undying…"

An undying love. Did it die?

"It did."

You spoke of her as something divine. A messiah you called her.

"And she was."

And the love of this messiah died. Did her love for you die? Or is it yours for her which died?

"Well, first off, I don't know that I was ever really loved. Not now once we are getting into dissecting it."

But you did love her?

"With a strength and purity that only a boy can feel. Ha! The eyes of a Retriever! Have you ever looked into their eyes?"

I have.

"And what did you see?"

I saw the earnest desire to please and to be loved and protected. What do you see?

"I see my reflection. I was the brown-eyed boy with a love great enough for that one owner that I could conquer the world."

She earned this love of yours?

"She must have."

Do you know how?

"With her touch. With her words. The first time I lay down with her, she saw the scars on my thighs and she cried while she made love to me, telling me no one would ever hurt me that way again. That it was those scars that compelled her to possess me – that she might show me what a gentle touch did to light a fire in my soul."

But she left you. For lack of words more accurate, more specific to the actual experience and all of its nuances and intricacies, she left you.

"She destroyed me."

This destruction, what did it look like?

"It looked like the fire of Hades licking at my eyes and my ears and my throat and my genitals; it blackened out my vision and left me stumbling through a darkness so absolute that I had no sense of spatial proximity to even my own limbs; it burned my ears so that all I could hear was every love song she ever sang me. I hear it still. It scorched my throat so that my voice became one stifled scream of her name that reverberated for years inside of my marrow; it branded my thighs so that no rape was greater, even should they all be combined, than the loss of my innocence so extreme as the smell of him on her skin."

That is the internal vision of the destruction. What was the outward image?

"It was an exhausted weeping. It was an illness of the mind that compelled me to drink and drug. The destruction seemed to exist directly in a center of me that cannot be defined or reached by any event since. I cannot travel there, nor can others, to place gentle hands of healing or to speak to and meditate. It was maybe a place that she created, so

69

she alone can unlock and enter? I'm not sure. It seems to have become a place of non-existence, like a story told for millennia, passed down as truth but vanished before the eyes of all. All that remains are archaeological debris that suggest its former status."

And some of that evidence is an outward image of the destruction.

"I ended up in psychiatric care, like a revolving door, over and over again, I would go into the ward, I would stay for a while I would leave. Inevitably, someone would find me in terrible shape; unable to eat or drink, even the booze. Stammering instead of speaking. Near comatose instead of sleeping. All of my equilibrium was set off on jagged kilter. And I would return to the psych ward."

Do you wonder why?

"'Why' what?"

Do you wonder why it impacted you to such a degree?

"No."

No, you don't wonder why?

"No. I do not wonder why. To wonder why can only come from one who does not know the feeling of having no safety in this world, of being entirely vulnerable and without the want to live in such an evil place but lacking the will to accomplish the deed of taking one's own life. How to explain to the uninitiated what joy comes from finding faith and trust and security in a world in which these very things I've mentioned did not exist? She gave me life. She painted me a universe that was all and only for me and I was safe and I was happy and I was free. My footing was founded in her. She was my only anchor. She took me away from this world…I'm struggling to find the words."

You are trying to speak of a language so very few but you have known. A struggle to articulate is to be expected.

"Imagine, if you can, being the only person on a planet inhabited by a hostile species. You are in costume, dressing up for a part, but they sense you. You move a little differently, you sound a little strange, you are found out. They beat you, they tie you, they burn you, whip you, gag you. They bore holes into your mind and implant their sputum and vomit and defecation. They fill you with all that is vile and then pick you up and ask you to smile."

Grim.

"That is what the world had done to me."

And grimmer still.

"She took me away from all of that. When I say she was my savior, it is not for melodrama. It is the closest I can come to an accurate title for what she was to me. But it was a mirage. It was the most amazingly beautiful lie that has ever been told – and the outcome of having tasted this perfect fruit is that all evils that came before her, bare no impact as great as hers; for all of her good, in Her leaving, she laid down on me the burden of returning to my world with skin that was no longer thickened and apathetic – I lacked skin; I was all exposed nerves. A toothache dipped in acid."

You spoke earlier of catharsis. Is it this detritus you wish to purge?

"I don't know that it is so severe now – the sputum and vomit and defecation of the world – as it was for me then. It is true that my healing has been somewhat fraudulent; I had pushed her into the recesses of my mind, created a labyrinth of corridors for Her to hide behind, so that I could

71

hope to cope. But time, while it has not healed me, it has carved its mark, just the same as wind through canyons that carve paths through the mountains. I am grown. And more importantly, I have become aware of my victimization and in that, I have found a power."

Have you now established that you are her victim?

"A victim of Her's? No. I am not able to make that proclamation. It is complex and it is convoluted, I don't know how much story there is to tell, I have never told this much. Maybe, by the end, I will know."

So by stating your victimization has brought you power, you refer to the times you were made victim prior to your time with Her?

"Yes, and maybe some times after as well. But I need to clarify, I do not mean to say that having been made a victim I was given power. I mean I found a way to prevent my victimization, or to at least be aware of what the predator is keying in on."

This power…?

"I wondered, in looking back at my life, what made me prey for so many. It never made sense to me how so much could happen to one person. And it is that fact alone that dismisses the possibility of reincarnation from my spiritual beliefs…one person cannot be asked to suffer this amount and then come back for more! And I cannot possibly learn from each of my experiences; while being pummeled by the latest I was still reeling from the one before."

"I digress."

Is there a need to?

"…No. I'm ok. Huh, I'm ok. Alright, to be real, I'm okay-ish. This is what I think happens:

72

A child is born. In this case, the child will be me. Something bad happened to me, I was in my crib. Maybe that person did not mean to do something bad to that baby, but bad it was. And so that baby was left with a little mark upon it. A scar. The scar is small and it is discreet. Not many people notice the scar. As a matter of fact, only people who want to see the scar can see it there. And the people who want to see the scar are the bad people. They are the predators. They are the criminals and the vile.

Someone saw my little scar and I was still a child. The mark on me says to them, 'this is a victim, this is my prey.' And so something bad happened to me. No worse than the last and as I soon learned in life there is no sense trying to separate degrees of bad – the next bad person will decide that for me.

And so I am marked and my mark grows bigger and bolder and more evident and more colorful and it is pronounced further with each bad that comes my way. Eventually, of all the people in the room, I am inevitably the next victim because my mark, my little scar, became a banner and that banner grew to be a beacon, and that beacon became a flashing marquee sign that advertised 'Easy Prey now playing,' and on the loudspeaker it shouted 'take this one, no one is watching, no one will stop you'…"

You mentioned a power, did I miss it?

"In so many words, I didn't actually say it. The power is this: I know what they see. So I hide."

Where do you hide?

"In my mind. It's a large space; I do not feel claustrophobic. As a matter of fact, sometimes I get lost in my mind."

And do you ever find Her in there, during your travels?

"No, she finds me. And that is when I get really lost."

How do you find your way back?

"Shouldn't I tell you where she takes me?"

Yes. Yes, that is the logical order; first where she takes you.

"She takes me to the school."

The high-school?

"Go-Lions! Yes, she takes me to the high-school and I am a boy again. It's a time warp and I am fully and completely my former self. I have no sense of the person I am today. I am all and only the fourteen, fifteen, sixteen, or seventeen-year-old me."

What do you do there?

"I search for her. She has called to me; I know I have lost her but I don't know how it happened or where we last were."

Are people there with you?

"Sometimes. Sometimes I am alone. And I know deep down that she is leaving. That she may even already be gone."

When there are others, who are they?

"Um…ahhh. There is a groaning of my soul. This has become so hard again. I am now pukey and my head spins. I've made mistake."

What's the mistake?

"Earlier today. I…"

What happened earlier today?

"I looked for her."

In your mind?

"No. Online."

And how did that feel?

"It feels as I feel now. A mangled car wreck. Confused. Unsure. I feel as though I have made a mistake."

What's the mistake?

"I think I've brought her into my world."

And where do you believe she was before?

"In my mind. Isolated to my dreams and the intermittent visits when the wind blows that certain way or the radio plays that certain song…like last night, it hits me in the gut and I physically experience the dread of knowing that she exists, Whitney Houston playing 'I Will Always Love You.' This must be so fucking boring for you. It sounds so childish and petty to cry over a song that a lover dedicated to you."

Is it petty to grieve?

"Have I grieved?"

Have you?

"Unceasingly. But not fully. Grief has done its dance like a twisted half-decayed zombie might dance. No, I haven't really grieved. I've coped and I've survived."

Are you ready to grieve?

"I don't know what there is to grieve. I don't know what happened to me."

Tell me about the song…

"We were in the back parking lot of Traverse. Across from the wheelchair ramp, there is a portable. I slept under the stairs to that portable a few times. When everyone seemed crazy and I couldn't bear to be near them; that was before she left Jim. She was in the driver's seat of her van, a green Ford Aerostar Sport, with the 'sport' written in a darker green and a stripe carrying on along the lower portion of the van doors to the rear bumper. The license plate was customized, it said, 'Titan'; a play on her husband's last name and nickname she said he had been given. She was crying, she played me the song while I stood at the door beside her, my hand on her knee, confused and scared, she told me if ever we couldn't be together to think of this song, she would be thinking of me.

And there is a lump in my throat now that is born of guilt. I become a child again and I am lonely for her. Ha. But don't worry, that guilt and fear and loneliness is soon replaced by reality and I am just mad. I'm almost entirely just mad. I hope, I hope so hard that she hears that song and she suffers over me. That she drowns in guilt the way that I drown in confusion. Because I guess a part of me thinks she really did fuck me up and she did a bad…"

She did what?

"I am so tired. I am beginning to feel resigned. As I said, I think today was a mistake, looking for her online. Finding her online. I wonder if telling this is really OK for me to do. I feel so tired and weak. I don't want to forget that I am not the same now as I was then, I am grown and strong. I am in love. I am focused and accomplished. And I know I said I was in love, but I am in love still after just about seven years with a little red-headed vixen. So I think I should just put this to bed. I shouldn't have woken this beast."

Do you really believe you woke Her?

"I believe by doing this, I am allowing Her into my present."

Wasn't she with you anyways?

"In dreams. And songs. And autumn breezes."

And that was OK for you?

"I thought it had to be. I thought that was as good as it would get. I did therapy, hard-core, for more than six years after. I thought I had healed as much as I could."

And is that good enough for you?

"It seems as though She is persisting of late. The dreams are becoming more. More often, more vivid and more real when I wake. I am having a hard time leaving my dream in the bed; I walk through the hours of the morning wondering which world I am in. Am I here, in this house white with black trim? On this street, tree-lined with beds of yellow scattered at their roots, leaves once green having subsided into a crisp death, the corpses now resting and soon to be scattered by North-Western? Am I really here and living? Or am I here and waiting and will soon be returning to the school? To the apartment on Fern street? To be happy there? Or to be tormented by the acknowledgment of her leaving? So, no. It wasn't really OK for me and it is definitely not OK for me now. But still, I am frightened."

Of, while not bringing her to life, of bringing her to light?

"Yes. That's it. Of bringing Her into the light and having to live inside that shadow it casts."

Do you assume that once she has been brought into the light that is where she will remain?

"Hum. Yes. Yes, that is what I am afraid of."

Again, I remind you, you spoke of catharsis. Perhaps once fully exposed the power of 'Her' will fade into gray and you will have no shadow to stand within?

From my Facebook message box:

I shouldn't do this. Talk about Pandora's Box. This is not planned.

I wish I knew who you were. I wish I knew who I was to you. If only I knew what happened to me…what formed my life and made me who I am today – for all the good and for all the torture. I am so happy to see you and your girls looking so well. But I should wish that more for myself than I do for you. Yet still, after so very many years and so many pains, I want only good for you. Even though it shreds me apart and rapes my soul. If there is kindness in you, please can you tell me what happened?

I am such a strong and independent man now, but I weep while I write this. Carrie, I loved you with such fierceness and with purity you may never have known, had it not been for the eyes of your children – we are the same, such utter adoration of your infants. I want to tell you I hate you and make you suffer for all my losses. Oh, how you scarred me and annihilated my spirit. Yet my dreams at night consist of finding you again. I am so in love with such a good woman but I am not complete; you still hold the essence of me and I wish I could have it back. Maybe you never meant wrong. Perhaps you didn't mean to hurt me and make me such a pathetic victim; lost. But maybe you did and how can I know? I wonder if there were others aside from me. If more were 'special.' Was I your secret Love?

Carrie, I have searched my entire life after you to find freedom. It is such strangeness to try to comprehend our past. Like an unreality that haunts me. You are my ghost. This is a small world now; the cyber ties that bind global communities. Perhaps, in the back of your mind, you expected this message to someday find you. Maybe you have had confidential conversations with me in the privacy of your mind as I do with your ethereal image? By grace, have you considered freeing me?

Again, I remind you, you spoke of catharsis. Perhaps once fully exposed the power of 'Her' will fade into gray and you will have no shadow to stand within?

Chapter 11
Draw Me In

"I love her. The boy in me loves her so much it makes me want to split into a million fragments of dust so that I can flow through the atmosphere and find my way back inside of her. To be breathed in by Her. To rest again in her breath. To lay down softly on her chest. To be inside of her and sheltered. To be absorbed by her and sheltered forever."

Do you think you would stay in her forever? If you were a fine mote of dust that she breathed in, would she not then also breathe you out?

"Even better! To be captured by her again and again, to feel the swell of her ribs as I journeyed inward, and the rush of her scented breath pushing me out as though she knew she was releasing me only to draw me in again – maybe this time deeper. To float for eternity in waves of her inhalation and exhalation, and for precious moments – wait for it! – to be hovering just before fine features of her face. Ecstasy."

Chapter 12
Of Pity or Hate

"I feel rather matter of fact right now. Do I hate Her? No, I don't think so. Maybe I even almost pity her. I've never been in this mindset before. Actually, I am sort of shocked to hear what I'm saying. Why would pity her? What am I fucking thinking? You see, this is what I mean about being scared. There is so much happening inside my mind and I can't keep up. I say something I never even knew I thought and I'm caught off guard. What can I anticipate? How do I predict the outcome so that I can prepare for this? It is like I'm in a foreign body – this is not mine, I am not this awake or alert, I have never been this focused and singular in my thoughts of Her. They have always been nagging at the back of my white matter. Now, synapsis are firing and messages are being sent and it wasn't me who posed the question or even had a thought of the question – where the hell could this be going? Do I hate her?"

Might it do some good to take a moment to breathe deeply?

"Was I not breathing?"

To speak, you were breathing. To feel the air moving within you, bringing vital energy and sustaining life? No.

"I will.

I have.

I suppose it could all be going in any number of directions, and at this point, it doesn't yet matter. It does no good to attempt to understand something before you have experienced it. That is an impossibility…"

You were speaking then, of perhaps not hating her, and maybe even pitying her…

"Right. And maybe I could pity her for the same reason that I don't particularly feel as though I hate her. That reason though would be based on a premise that what we had, the love we 'shared' – you know what, I'm just going to say the love I had for her I know was real, I don't know that she loved me though, but I will assume that to be true for this premise alone. If it was real, then I don't hate Her. I really couldn't hate someone for loving me could I?"

Couldn't you?

"I'm not going there right now. And so I wouldn't hate her, I don't hate her. And I'm sad for her because as a mother maybe she had to go back to her husband, the father of her children. Those little girls deserve only happiness. Their parents, Her and Jim, gave them so much better than I could have. So if she loved me, I cannot hate her for leaving, because as a mother, she *should* have. I loved those girls. I'm glad they had their dad. And if she loved me and she left me, then I feel sorry for her because she had to be without my love and instead have him."

So in the end, there was only a boy. All alone. Severed from love and the god of gods.

"There was a short time after she 'left' that I believed if I expressed enough pain, she would come back. Of course, she would come to see that she was wrong to leave; a decision she made in fear and misdirected loyalty."

I remember the day I recognized that this was not so. And in that knowing I came to a clarity of understanding.

An orange Toyota supra, grinding through the gears, an angry type of focus with a layer of calm to quell its burning fury that would have let me jerk the wheel hard to the right to direct its horse-power to break through the metal railing that lined the corner of the highway so that I might plummet, cold and hard, into the dirty waters that lurked thick and heavy beneath the bridge. It could have been quite fitting – to drive through that barricade and be swallowed up by the stink and rot of the sewage that flowed into the water treatment plant for filtration and then releases into the Fraser River.

But that was not the plan. I had an element of control and so I would exercise it.

Hougan Park. The place where we made love so often, the place we would lay in the grass and speak our dreams while glancing up at the big sky. It's a long driveway flanked by a lazy width of water to the north and full old trees to the south. There are concrete buildings, windowless and small. They are outhouses and they are places that housed our secret adventures.

I went there in mourning on this particular day. I went there with a purpose.

The night was early and darkness cloaked me and my tear-stained sorrow. I stepped out, calm and slow. Understood. I flipped forward the driver's seat to gain access to my hose in the back seat. It was really easy. A length of hose and duct tape. I attached it to my tailpipe, engine thrumming.

I looked around. I took it in. Every memory living and breathing, the sound of her in the rustle of the tree branches, the feel of her, the warm wind that whipped up around me; excited. The taste of her was just slightly out of reach but my taste buds recalling: the cherry Chapstick, the peach gum, the vanilla of her perfume like acid on my mouth when I kissed and licked at her breasts and cleavage. And in that remembering, in that feeling of her? Then I understood.

I cannot live a life unknowing of her love.

I got in the car and closed the door.

Was there music playing? I don't know. But a song is on my mind right now. The song that played on the radio the day in Passage when the phone rang and the hospital said, 'it is time.' No Doubt singing, "Don't Speak....

I suppose I wanted them to find me clean and sleeping. That's why I chose the poisoning in the car."

Chapter 13
Apartment #12

"I was in bed. It was a large room with a queen bed along the wall opposite the door. And a door that leads to the small patio and green area allotted to us.

We made love on the floor the night before, between the side of the bed and the exterior wall with the large window. We did that because the, *Her*, girls were home. And if they woke to a sound unfamiliar and came to the room, they would not be shocked and seized by confusion at what they saw.

That morning, lying in bed, awake, I had my head turned to the right and I watched Her down the little hall between the bedroom closets that led to the ensuite bathroom.

I caught her. She was bleaching her upper lip. Now, if a boy can see that and still think of only beauty…"

Chapter 14
Counseling

"Ashten. Ashten? Are you here with me?" My eyes are at the window looking over the parking lot. "Yes." But she knows I mustn't really be. She says, "Tell me five things you see." Slow to respond, it takes time to separate the pieces from the whole, to find edges in the fog of my view that can make sense to vision. "I see cars. I see your car. I see Rose's car. I see the dumpster."

"Tell me five things you hear," I am told.

"I hear you. I hear cars on the road. I hear the noise canceller. I hear you. I hear you."

"Tell me five things you feel," I am told.

"I feel…the chair. I feel the chair at my ass. I feel the chair at my knees. I feel the chair at my back."

"Tell me four things you see," I am urged onward. But my gaze is not ready to come inside yet today. I'm not ready to be in this room. I'm not ready to look up and see Her face transplanted onto this person and know what I am here for. I'm not ready to see reality. I'll just stay in the parking lot today. With my body in this building, up the stairs to the second floor, past the patio with glass and aluminum railing, a right turn at the end of the hall, and a right once more to get me through the door into the waiting room and then past the secretaries' desk and into your office. I'm not ready today. I will let my mind stay outside.

But I say: "I see cars. I see the sky…" it frightens me, the sky. I don't like to look at it anymore. Especially at night. I don't look at it anymore at all. Not without an immediate panic attack. The vastness of it? Is it loneliness that comes to me when I see the infinite depths of black? I don't know. I feel only panic without any thought. I look downward. I have accidentally come into the room. "I see my feet. I see the carpet, I see the edge of the table."

"Now four things you hear," I am compelled to come further into the room. Into the now.

"I hear you, Margaret."

"I hear the white noise," the noise canceller for privacy. "I hear me talking. I hear the cars. I hear a door close. and I know the next thing I will feel. It won't be the type of 'feel' she wants me to identify. Those which she wants me to identify are the external things, the tangible, the touchable, the solid formed molecules. But instead, after I heard that door open, I know I will feel the door inside me open. It will hurt so very, very badly.

'Four things you feel,' I am told.

I feel my shattered psyche clinging to a shard of truth. I want to take that shard and work it under my nail. I want to force it into my nail bed and hold it safe there, letting it burn and ache and throb. Oh, that a piece of pain might be embedded in me to exist as the reminder of the smallest of truths – She is gone and I am alive. And I don't want to be. I acquiesced. 'I feel the chair at my back. I feel the chair under my legs. I feel the chair at my knees. I feel the breeze

87

from the window.' It's not high up. Not worth a jump. But to go through that window and hear and feel and see the glass chunk away past my hurtling body until my mass is disintegrated into the atmosphere. That would be a moment I could live within.

'Tell me three things you see.' I am urged further still.

'I see the window. I see the frame of the windows. I see the parking lot below.'

'Tell me three things you hear.' I am almost here entirely now. More than I want to hear. There is a screaming on repeat and it tracks in looping circles on a black screen behind my forehead. My skull actually gets thick with it. I *feel* it there. Behind the scream, there is a keening wail – I think it is me. And under it all, the percussion and the pipes, there is a chorus of all Her words. Words of love; spoken and lied. 'I hear you. I hear me. I hear the cars.'

'Tell me three things you feel.' Margaret, calm and persistent.

'I feel the chair at my back. I feel the chair at my thighs,' these are always the first ones I say and they are almost always true when I say it. But this time I have not made it to the part when I tell her that I feel my feet on the floor, 'I feel my hands on the armrests.' The fabric chairs have wooden arms and they end in a curl of a discreetly carved downward turn, I grip that like the safety bar on a roller coaster. Or an airplane losing its attempt to defy gravity as it rapidly descends through the clouds headed for the hard impact of earth.

We do this, called, '5,4,3,2,1,' until I claim one thing I see, Margaret; one thing I hear, me; and one thing I feel, my feet on the floor.

And then she says, 'Hello Ashten.'

'Hi, Margaret.'

'How have things been?'

We do this multiple times a week. It's like eating and drinking. It's the way I stay alive. For seven years."

Chapter 15
Blood in Black Darkness

It's been a while.

"It has. I've been…unwell."

Unwell, how so?

"Like before. Like at the beginning."

At the beginning of…?

"Like at the beginning of the madness that overtook me."

And She was the madness? We are still speaking of that?

"We are. At the beginning of the madness…"

Sorry, I will interrupt here. The beginning of the madness was the start of…the relationship?

"Is that what we are calling it? A relationship? I suppose that is fine for now. To call it that, to call the undefined by a name has to happen, everything must be categorized. I suppose that is the case with this too. This definition is the reason for the process of telling, in so many ways. But no, the madness I refer to now is what happened at the immediate end of the 'relationship.'

There was constant anticipation of death. It went beyond a wanting of death. There was a part of me that warred against death – duplicity because a great long sleep was what I so often, daily craved. But this anticipation was a torment. It teased the fibers of my brain and distorted all my senses. My chest would live in the moment of a heart attack; the pain swelling in my chest with an ache and a burn, my heart squeezing in exhausted contractions and I could feel it fail and I knew that I was dying. I *knew* I was dying. My head would pound until my vision blurred; blood in black darkness swirling until I was blind and a clot would disengage and stop my brain from telling my body to live. It was not a thought or a fear. I *knew* it was happening, on the verge of death. All of this I felt – a palpable knowledge that I was going to, at this very moment, die. And despite how badly I wanted to escape the world and my reality I raged against the end in mortal fear."

And this happens for you again now?

"Not exactly like this. But near enough to call it the same version of insanity."

Chapter 16
A Fugue State

You are back. How is today going?

"On January 23, 2018, I phoned the Edmonton City police station."

That's what, two days ago?

"Two days ago, yes."

And you phoned the police. Tell me about that.

"I asked the person who took my call how one would go about reporting a crime that had been committed. I explained the crime occurred in a different province. They suggested I contact the police of that city. And so I did."

What was that like for you?

"It was like a fugue state; my limbs moved, my mouth spoke, my tears flowed, yet, I was strangely quiet inside and out."

And what did you discuss with them?

"Not much. Not at first, but the next day, January 24, a constable from the Abbotsford police made contact with me at 10:08 a.m. I gave a brief statement. I wrote it down on paper in preparation for the call:

In November of the year I was fourteen I entered into a sexual relationship with my school counselor. *I am robotic as I say this. I am in awe of myself.* It lasted until the August before my seventeenth birthday. 'Her name was...' and I spelled the name because I still cannot say it out loud, *like this: First name, C.A...last name, T.I...*He read it back to me, the name, and I said yes, that is Her name."

Chapter 17
The Bringing Back of Existence

Why do you call this, what happened to you and unreality?

"Because that's the way I've been living. In an unreality, it is mine alone, existing only for me. Only with me."

But it is real. Real, as in, it has happened.

"Yes. In that sense it is real."

Can I challenge your words then?

"Challenge them? For what purpose?"

To take them, and thereby the experience, into the realm of what we classify as reality. So that you might then come to a place where you can speak of it, express it, and find a home for it in the light of tangibility.

"I don't see it as something tangible. Not the sensations or the images or the worm-wood etchings on my soul and psyche."

Define what is tangible.

"In my idea of it, it requires a solidity, a concreteness to it."

And to be tangible, as many see it, means that there is a material or physical realness to it.

"Right. Right, I see what you are suggesting."

Do you?

"I think so. The real part of it – the tangible part of it exists in the past. It existed then; the shared touches, the words spoken, the rent paid on the apartment on Fern Street."

And what of the times you wake from a dream – what of that sensation? When you remember the smells, the tastes, the feel of flesh along flesh. That is palpable?

"So you suggest that even in this present moment when my mind calls to life the nerves of my flesh, that this too is tangible?"

Does it fit for you?

"It is true that there is a physical and visceral knowledge of what has existed. So in definition, I see that it is tangible. And in that sense then, it is a reality. But what lacks is the *concrete*. The solid and absolute acceptance that it is truth."

You are allowing us to get deeper into the crux of this all. You seek the acceptance of truth. Is that your greater purpose in this process?

"Yes! It is to have the truth heard and for that truth to be accepted."

Who is it that needs to accept it?

"It is me. I need to accept it. I need to call it by name and define it."

Who else needs to accept it?

"She does. He does. They all do."

Who?

"She, Her, the woman I gave my breath and heartbeat to. The woman who raped my soul and left me absent of existence beyond her reach."

Who else.

"Her husband."

Why him?

"So that he might know the truth."

What benefit does him knowing the truth bring?

"Isn't knowing the truth and benefit enough? Isn't knowing the full extent of a person's motivation and actions what we deserve as a person?"

So you hope to benefit him? That is what you are saying.

"No. I do not care to benefit him. Does the truth need to benefit the hearer of the spoken facts? Can it not just be that I might be vindicated by the truth being known?!"

So you have grown the purpose then. You want the truth to be known and you want this knowledge to vindicate you?

"Yes."

And what do you need to be vindicated for?

"I don't know. You are confusing me."

You were confused already.

"You tire me. And at the same time excite my mind, you are steering me into words I had not known existed in my brain."

You knew. But you dug them deep and thought they might be buried away. What do you need to be vindicated for?

"For going crazy. For giving up on life. For being the kid that no one believed."

Did they not believe you?

"No."

Did you give them a chance to?

"That's not fair!"

'Fair' is a four-letter word that starts with 'F.'

"Fuck, as in, fuck you. That is the four letter word you're thinking of."

It is time to push you. Tell me, did you give them a chance to believe you?

"Some of them."

And as for the others?

"The good of the one versus the good of the many."

A noble idea. But how does it fit here?

"It is why I never told."

Who was the one?

"I was."

Who gave you that interpretation?

"Raphael."

Do you have a sense of why?

"Then I believed, as you mentioned, in nobility. But now, I wonder if that was for self-preservation. His. And maybe Her's too."

So you never told.

"No. As a matter of fact, I did more than not tell – aside from Meryl and even then I don't know that I said Her name. When I spoke to the police, I told them that nothing happened. They countered with what Meryl had reported. I told them, a woman investigator, that I did not wish to pursue anything. There were the girls to think of on top of my loyalty to this divine figure we had created in her."

Another large statement. You recognize that you created this divinity in her and that it was not really who She was?

"I don't know. I don't know. Speak slowly to me. I am having a hard time comprehending, keeping up with the evolution of all of this."

Who were the many?

"Come again?"

The good of the one versus the good of the many...

"Oh." And a smile spreads. "They were the girls. I knew them from the little one's second birthday till her fourth and some months beyond. And the eldest, looking so much like her mother, from around four years old up to her sixth birthday, a party held at, 'Dino Town.' A theme park in the outer reaches of the Valley. And then again some months past that."

They were the many?

"Yes. And tied up in there was Her."

"So in keeping your silence, you hoped to benefit the many; Her and the children?"

"Yes. And I suppose so many others too. Mary Kay Letourneau; I believed then in her love for the boy whose child she carried. And for Raphael – he had some of my faith too. Some of my belief that a man, a human, could be good and only slightly flawed and therefore need not stand accountable for having allowed the love to blossom right in front of his eyes."

You have named a few people. These are the many you hoped to benefit – to protect?

"Yes."

And how do you reconcile this protection of them, by way of keeping your secret, defending the events, with the now? With coming to a place where not only do you speak your history but you claim a desire to share it with a broader audience, so to speak?

"Reconciliation is complicated. You are right. How can I have this noble ideology and then spit against it and release the torrents of my thoughts and memories?"

Does the ideology fit still?

"Did it ever? Did I take man's word, Raphael's, and twist them into my own? Making a circle fit a square peg? All for the sake of self-preservation?"

A worthy question.

"If I had not known that phrase, would I have done differently? I do not know. But what I do know is that I strove to live a selfless life, one in which I harmed none, gave back to the world none of the evils I had known. I would protect those who needed protection. I would sacrifice myself so that those worthier than me could excel and achieve and survive. In going against Raphael's words, the good of the one versus the good of the many, I would have been selfish. He gave me those words. It is an awful painful brain that I use now to attempt to calculate why he gave them to me. Why at the time of the flood gates opening and the truth threatening to be revealed did he choose to place me in a glass box from which I viewed the world isolated from them – speechless and inert?"

So now, what of the good of the one?

"I am the one. I have been the one and the alone for more than two decades. I struggle at this moment to see the valor in that."

And this allows you to finally speak?

"The girls are grown. When last I saw the eldest was getting married, maybe married already by now. And Tes…and the youngest, she is not young in the sense of a minor. Perhaps now they do not need my protection.

Though I wish I could shelter them from this truth, I find it easy, at this moment in time, to say that I cannot sacrifice myself for them. They do not know me. They do not love me. They did not get the wrapped birthday presents and the helium balloons that I left on the doorstep of the pale peach house on Denman street when they were little and after she left. She packed them up in Her van and drove them to the school, telling me it was inappropriate to give them gifts or come to her home."

And Raphael, you said he was of the many...

"I owe him nothing. He gave me a bent view on how to handle the torture I endured. He benefitted himself well enough, no need for me to benefit him also. I will not go out with the intent to harm but I will not harbor the secret sorrows of my youth so that he might not feel a moment – any number of moments – of discomfort."

So then, this is the tangible.

"I will bring it to their doorsteps. There is no return address this time. They cannot package it up and lay it back at my feet. If they choose, they can put it in the dumpster – someone else will find it. They can tuck it into a locked cabinet – instead of in my mind, they will house the secret. They can burn it in the flames – it will be carried up into the ether and released to so many more; cinder and ashes feeding the soil of the earth and taking root more deeply as real. One day, they will come to know that like I, they cannot escape it."

Chapter 18
Baptized

"There were days in the sun. There were warm days in the glorious sun where the sky and the soil and the water and Her and I all became one; baptized in Her arms. They were days of magnificent youth. Do you understand the impact when I say 'magnificent'? I wonder if you can know the wonder of it all."

Magnificent. A word used often elicits a sense of profound beauty and extravagance.

"Used too often, yes. Used to describe events that are far too mundane to warrant its use. When I say 'magnificent' I mean it in its most complete version. And yet, still it does not scrape the surface of my memory of feelings for Her and for those days."

Tell me more about these days.

"They were the glory days of youthful bliss. We would go to the wilderness where we did not have to hide our love away. Her clothes would be off and the shadows of towering trees would tattoo Her skin painting Her as a goddess of Pan. We made love and the already hot skies would open wider to expel the source of all light and warm us until we were giddy with heat and we would retreat to the stream to refresh our skin and make love again."

There was Irish whiskey in smoked crystal glasses on our first night in the apartment together. The first time we made love in a bed.

There was so much good. So much beauty and what I believed, and so I will call, purity in our love and our lovemaking. She was my first. My first drink of alcohol in a real glass, my first lover. And I think now, I didn't need a lover, I needed a mother. I needed a protector. I needed a teacher. And those last two things were what she was supposed to be. What she was employed to be. And I think she must really have loved me to lay so much on the line and now, I feel guilty and ridden with it, the guilt, for starting this process, feeling these feelings, remembering these memories and feeling as though they were all and only good and so why am I torn up and devastated inside? Devastated: shocked with grief.

Oh! for those long days in the sun! Warm days in the glorious sun where the sky and the soil and the water and Her and I all became one; baptized in Her arms. Excruciate.

Chapter 19
A Screaming Head Turning-In-Mad-Spinning-Circles

"I touched the essence of life. The womb of the woman. My fingers tingled, no, they hummed and they vibrated as though they were scepters pulsing with power. When I removed my hand from between her thighs and looked down to see her blood in lines down to my knuckles filling the creases of my joints, I looked in awe from them to her face. I felt a swell of loving passion and an urge to hold onto her in an embrace that I prayed would not end.

I saw blood long after She was away from me. The blood began to flow. In my mind, it became a life source. One of my own. A gift she had given. A holy sacrifice that the nerves of my fingers might never shake the vision of.

In a mall, I was walking. I was there, but not really there. My body was. And my hand was held by a child's hand.

And the hallucination, which I didn't know was a hallucination came:

I looked up from the child's hand; that was real, to see the crowds of people passing us by, they too were real.

Their eyes looked at me. They were hard eyes. I don't think I would call them mean, just hard. They had a stare to them that looked into me but not past, not through me. They had a stare that met my soul. And as they came closer, their eyes, never leaving mine, began to bleed. They welled up and spilled fine rivulets of ruby blood. That part was not real. But it was real to me. Frantic I looked from person to person. Many dozens of them in a procession moving past me; their faces took on the characteristics of the mourning. And from their eyes – bloody tears.

I called the name of the child whose hand I was holding (also real). Three years old, she looks up at me. Large, blue, crystalline eyes. They pooled full of blood until there was no white left to be seen. And the blood spilled in rivers down her cheeks. The blood came out black from her nose. She talked to me, words I don't recall, and the black blood stretched across her lips, gooey and thick, filling her mouth and making her words a gagging sound. All of that blood, red and slick and shinning from her eyes melded into the black dead blood that drooled from her mouth.

It's been a while because, as I said, I haven't been well. And like I said before then, during the earlier times of the telling, I am not a psychiatric case. Not like my mother. Not like the mean and spiteful, unaware, unconcerned, unremorseful type of psychiatric that courses through the synapsis of the deranged. But it seems, as much as I have fought for healing, it seems I too am now in a state of psychiatric distress."

And today, you are well enough to be here? Having this exchange?

"How to know for sure? How to decide when to delve into the complex content of Pandora's Box?"

Tell me about Pandora.

"It is a piece of Greek mythology. But in this day and age, we use it as an idiom to express the event of releasing great and unexpected sorrows. It is presented as a gift...but in all of its perceived glory, it really is a curse. Once opened, all of the troubles escape and cannot be recaptured; cannot be packaged up and returned to the sealed box where it remains inert."

And yet you are here.

"I am. I am all here. No portion left in the faded shadows, wrapped in shrouds to protect the essence. I am fully here. I am alive and in this moment."

And you want to tell me what has been happening?

"I will tell you. I will tell you that I hallucinated again."

A scary thing to experience.

"Ah, but I feel perhaps as though I have come to a place of indifference. I am not sure that it frightens me, this going crazy, this state of being between two worlds and being vacuumed into the next. Into the insane. I used to be so afraid of being crazy. And now, now I wonder if it would be a restful place. I would not know, right? I would have no sense of being crazy. There would be no effort, no reaching, and no panicked desire to retain a hold on what is defined as reality."

We see the insane as a suffering sort.

"Yes, but is that our own projection? The projection of the seemingly sane. Is that not really us, those of us with a firm hold on reality that gives that suffering nature to the insane?" A laugh. A bitter sound. "Isn't it us?! Those with a sense of firm fucking reality, those of us who, as I said were grasping for reality, a firm hold if you will…isn't it us who are beyond what the human brain can fucking manage?!"

We all manage what we can.

"Well then, dear fucking sir. I do not manage! I do not manage. I am in an unmanageable state. Oh, give me drugs, not for fun or for beautiful and temporary disillusionment. Give me drugs to drag me back into the realm of the masses. The population that sees and hears and feels all things as a collective, the realness of that – isn't it only real because the majority claims it to be?!"

You are in a dark place. I see this.

"What do you see? What sight, human and fickle and dependent on past experience, dependent on a life history and text books and the words of mothers and fathers and teachers and the people anonymous and passing by tells you what to see – what do you see? And what do you hear? Do you hear the stink and vile anger, lacking in desperation, sure of my righteousness – do you hear? What darkness do you catch a glimpse of? You, who are uninitiated into this realm of sorrow and suffering? You!

You.

Are.

A.

Fraud.

More.

Than.

I.

Am.

I dare you to speak. I dare you to say what you think you see!"

How do you bear it?

"Ha! I do not bear it! I am…lost in it. I am a screaming head turning in mad spinning circles. So give me drugs!"

Did they give you drugs?

"Ah, they did. They gave me drugs – antipsychotics. Antipsychotics. Oh, they think it will quell the beast. It will silence the unreal callers who speak my name and call my attention to them only to then disappear.

They vanish after they have called my eyes to lay upon them. They speak in a language only I can hear. So, is it me who has gone crazy, crazy, crazy. Or is it you who are deaf to the voices that are real, that exist beyond the decibels of your sheltered ears?"

I am wondering…

"Do not interrupt me. Not now. Not when the hate flows like lava erupting from Vesuvius. Not when my mind is so keen. Not when my soul is so filled with the bitter excrement that I have no choice – or, actually, choice it might be – to speak and reveal the thoughts of my innermost.

I heard a voice. It called my name. I know it is not her because it is a name She has never called before."

How is it that she never before called you your name?

"I changed it, after Her. I don't go by that same name anymore. There are so many reasons why. First, and most truly, I had to give myself a name by which I could be called that reflected who I am. And if I hadn't – imagine then! If another were to call me by those same sounds and syllables,

I might drown and be lost in the fantasy of Her. I changed my name."

I see.

"So I heard my name. Someone called it. It didn't sound like Her. I don't know whose voice it was. But I spun in circles and asked those near me who it was that said my name. None of them had."

Chapter 20
Expanded

"A strange sensation would overtake my mouth. In the space under the tongue where the tissue, heavy with blood vessels, meets the soft palate. It was a mixture of numbness and heaviness. If I were to compare it I would say it was as though my flesh expanded beyond the dividing lines of my actual flesh, as though from beneath my chin there was a piece of me that felt like nylon might feel if it were laden with a mass of metal balls."

Chapter 21
Walking Between the Worlds

"So, 'are you a lesbian?' she asks me. I hold her gaze, turned my eyes to a hard slant, 'And who the fuck are you to know...'

Yes, I recall this line. You mentioned this earlier.

'It seems to be something I would rather overlook. But I recognize its significance.'

A significance to your story?

'I suppose it is. There is a portion of this, that I will tell you, that is so tied up in Her.'

So what is it that you will tell me?

"That, on top of it all, I also happen to be transgender. I have walked between both worlds, never fully in either one. Never man nor woman but something in between, or beyond."

You are right. This is significant. How does it tie into Her?

"When we met, I was a girl. No, let me correct that. When we met, I was *called* a girl. I was young and tough and tumbled. From the time I was little, I wore blue-striped tube socks and a ball cap with pride. I stole my brother's clothes and I stuffed a sock in my underwear. I was all boy.

Except of course for the part where I was my mother's daughter."

But how does it tie into Her?

"There are two memories that stand out strongest in my mind. The first time we made love in a bed, She told me after, 'I didn't know how this would work, I didn't know how we would have sex.' I lay on top of Her, our bodies naked and slick with the sweat of passion and foreplay. I put my right arm along the lower portion of my body and I parted Her with my fingers, my hips undulating as the bone of my flesh careened into Her heat. The power mounted until She quivered beneath me."

That is the most graphic you have been.

"It's not that I want to be. It's that I feel I have to be. How else will you come to know what Her words mean and how they impacted me? I have to tell it all."

And how are you feeling now that you are telling this part?

"I am numb. I am separated from that time bodily. The hormone therapy has been at play for nearly two decades in my system and I have been reformed in so many ways. That is another reason I fear the memories will elude me – the testosterone injections have altered my chemistry and have put up a barrier between my now and my then. But I feel Her. A faint tingling at the tips of my fingers, a barely lucid recollection of Her warmth.

And She would tell me how masculine I am, how manly. That is what stands out. I had never told Her that I was, deep down on the inside, far back yet fully in my mind, a boy. And yet She knew to call me a Sweet Boy, a Strong Boy, Her Boy.

She is not the cause of this. I need that to be certain in your mind. The only cause is creation alone. Creation by whomever it is that you credit that creation to; a god and goddess, multiple gods, or a celestial bang that through some kind of happenstance initiated all existence. But I will tell you more about this some other time."

And why not more now?

"Because now you know what you need to know. Now you know the part that was about Her."

You didn't tell me very much.

"No. Because from what I have told you, you will draw conclusions. You will let it all marinate in your mind and you will come to understand the suggestion of its severity. The rest is for another time. For now, I feel as though I am in some kind of hurry, I want to keep going with the rest of my story."

Understood. If every story has a beginning and an end, are we coming to the end?

"You say that is the case, the beginning, and an end. But does this story have an end? I am not convinced that it does."

Then how will you carry on living in the same story? One that you do not want to live?

"It isn't even a story I created. It was written for me."

Have you not taken it over now? Are you not the one who progresses the story and defines its course?

Chapter 22
An End

You are back. How have you been?

"Contemplative."

And what is it you have been considering?

"The end. If we carry on with the premise that every story has a beginning and an end, then I suppose I must, at some point, come to an end."

And this end you are ready to share?

"I don't know that I can be ready. Not really. Not fully. And I don't know that this story has yet reached its end. I feel as though perhaps the end has been taken."

By whom?

"By the natural progression. You see, I had this story as my very own. My own excruciate to endure. But in that phone call on January 23rd, I seem to have relinquished a portion of my reality onto another...and they are now in control of the end I think."

How does that affect you?

"It is at once both good and bad. I know the police have spoken to people, interviewed them. They bore witness to my experience – this should be good, and relieving – but once again I am isolated. In holding it to myself, I was alone with it, the only one living it and so therefore isolated within the universe of its existence. And now, now that they are speaking, I am isolated once again. For as they speak I am not present, I do not know what they say, I do not get to know. They talk about me, without me. The world spins madly beyond not only my control but also beyond my conscious awareness. I am alone. And so, it is both good and bad. The event lives beyond me, shared by others with me, and that is the good."

Does the good outweigh the bad in this?

"In the knowledge, yes. In the experience? Well, that is still mine alone. Until more people hear."

You are willing now to let people further in? Into the end?

"Into *an* end, yes."

"Take me there…

The end. There was no end. Not of it. Not of Her. The end was mine. I was ended. There was an unraveling; it seemed that it both encompassed and simultaneously exposed all of me. All of me…how to explain that She created a depth in me that even I cannot comprehend. There is no location for this 'me.' It is my mind and my heart; it is my soul and every breath that my body heaves inward and releases jagged/crying/moans of excruciating loss. There is no way to define the extent of my aching torment. I know only that it was, and it is, the fullest sense of my entire being; the tangible and the intangible."

And of the relationship? The affair? There was an end to that.

"There was a car with a broken ignition switch and wires exposed to shock it to life. There was a hockey stick in the back hatch. And as the sun shone down on the road and the field and the block of wood and concrete and glass that was our home, I thought to use that stick on his skull."

Who is he? Whose skull?

"His. Jim's. The husband, father. The man who raped her.

So there is a day that I call the end. Understand, as I have said before, this is not the true end. That I cannot yet share as I do not know how the universe I shared with her will unfold."

Understood.

"The day I call the end happened on a summer day. The sky was so blue and the air so clear. I was ready for anything. Or so I thought."

Even in going this far in telling you, I have become nauseated and my mouth is pooling with the saliva that threatens the vomit after the retching. But the sky was blue and the air was clear and I was about to celebrate another day in the invigorating arms of my beloved.

She had the neighbors across the street watching the girls. I should have anticipated something different, something un-good about this day. That was a strange thing to do. Why send the girls to the neighbors? Why wouldn't I just be with them while she was out with Jim discussing, what she said to me, was the separation? Oh, my head. How it pounds under the pressure of this memory.

She came back to me. She came back to me smelling of him. I have to close my eyes just now and brace myself against the onslaught of the scent and the changed feeling in Her. I need comfort now. I will smoke a cigarette. I quit fourteen years ago but I will smoke one now. I will pull the heat into my mouth and let it burn as it travels past my throat and into my lungs stealing the breath from a scream waiting at the edge of my voice. You don't mind?

Your body is your house. This is your house. Do as you will. Do as you need.

"I need. I need. I need something undefined. Something so different than the feeling I felt when she said she held his hand. A betrayal so sharp and defined, so all-encompassing to leave me without a heartbeat. Oh! that I could have died just before that announcement, I would have died complete. And I would have transcended this earth knowing I was encapsulated in Her divine and ethereal embrace."

But you did not die.

"I did not die. I stood to suffer for decades gone by. In a torment worse than Satan's hell, a heat more torturous than his fiery lake. I think my soul would have solace there, anything would be better than this. Than that. I must remember I am not there right now. But I am so absorbed by the feeling – I live it again. I live it again and again and again. I torment, I suffer, I anguish. I excruciate.

Where do I go from here?"

You go all the way there.

"I don't know where 'there' is."

You do.

"It is in my lungs and my heart, in my fast-beating heart and the heat of the pulse that it sends throughout my being. 'There' is the place where no other can reside, where no other has been bidden. 'There' is the spot where torture reigns in its jagged mass of blackness and I find no release in the exhalation of my screaming sorrow.

She left me. She raised me and she left me. She taught me, she groomed me, and she tore the flesh from my bones, raping my soul and leaving me chaffed and covered in acid burns. She left me to rot in my vomit and defecation so that I became something putrid.

She kissed my inner being and bore me to a place of Her central sanctum where none could pass and no trespass could exist – but it was fantasy. A corrupt world that she fabricated around me until I was so dependent on her existence for my own that I was blissfully lost inside her eyes and her flesh. And so left starved and emaciated by Her absence.

She shattered me. At the side of the road, with her husband and the neighbors watching She said, 'You aren't as independent as I thought you were.' She said, 'This is a sin: living this way. You are a sinner,' She said to me.

And so I imploded. It was all me. I was all wrong. She told me. She told me and she wouldn't lie. She told me and so it had to be true. She told me and so I was left for dead."

Chapter 23
Where the Unknown Is Known

"You know, all of this time we've spent. I don't think I even understand who you are…"

You are the child; I am the man. You are the afflicted, I am the healed.

I am you.

We overcome.

Chapter 24
Excruciate Persists

"There has been a Preliminary Hearing. The Provincial Court heard three days of testimony. The ruling was in my favor – this now progresses to Supreme Court.

The charge is Sexual Exploitation – from September 1996 to September 1998.

My mind is racked by confusion and fear and sorrow."

As I said, we overcome.

"And yet, there is more to come."

Ingram Content Group UK Ltd.
Milton Keynes UK
UKHW022005130423
420127UK00014B/1247

9 781649 795939